"If You Turned into a Monster"

# "If You Turned into a Monster"

## Transformation through Play: A Body-Centered Approach to Play Therapy

*Dennis McCarthy*

*Foreword by Richmond K. Greene*

Jessica Kingsley Publishers
London and Philadelphia

First published in 2007
by Jessica Kingsley Publishers
116 Pentonville Road
London N1 9JB, UK
and
400 Market Street, Suite 400
Philadelphia, PA 19106, USA

*www.jkp.com*

Copyright © Dennis McCarthy 2007
Printed digitally since 2010

**Library of Congress Cataloging in Publication Data**

McCarthy, Dennis, 1951-
     If you turned into a monster : transformation through play : a body-centred approach to play therapy / Dennis McCarthy ; foreword by Richmond K. Greene.
     p. ; cm.
     Includes bibliographical references and indexes.
     ISBN 978-1-84310-529-9 (pbk. : alk. paper) 1. Play therapy. 2. Monsters in art. 3. Creation (Literary, artistic, etc.)--Therapeutic use. I. Title.
     [DNLM: 1. Play Therapy--methods. 2. Child. 3. Imagination. 4. Symbolism. WS 350.2 M123i 2007]
     RJ505.P6M364 2007
     618.92'891653--dc22

                                                                        2007008660

**British Library Cataloguing in Publication Data**
A CIP catalogue record for this book is available from the British Library

ISBN 978 1 84310 529 9

*Dedicated to Carol, Laena and Emma, who have helped me to better know my monster and myself.*

# Contents

Please call me by my true names so that I can wake up, and so the door of my heart can be left open, the door of compassion.

(Thich Nhat Hanh)

The essential requirement to cure psychic disturbances is the re-establishment of the natural capacity for love.

(Wilhelm Reich)

# Foreword

I recommend this book not only to therapists who work with children but especially to parents and teachers – in fact, to any of us who carry a wounded child within and are still seeking to free our passion and our spirit. All of you will be moved, drawn in, and catch a clear vision of what it is that most of us seek and yearn for, yet somehow due to the labyrinth of our growing up, lost touch with. For this book pushes past the complexities of psychological theory and jargon and speaks to the heart of the matter: the recovery of a child's connection to that vibrant, alive, inner center, what C.G. Jung called "the Self."

I have a clear memory of an evening in my own childhood in which I was being tucked into bed by my mother. Suddenly I burst into wrenching sobs, racked by a profound grief. My mother inquired with deep concern about what was upsetting me, but all words failed. I did not know for what I grieved. Only years later, somewhere in mid-life, I realized exactly what it was that lay behind that sorrow. I had become, early on, a pleasing and dutiful son, and lost the connection to my inner center as a result.

No matter how it occurs, this is the ultimate tragedy of childhood and the one to which Dennis McCarthy speaks. His therapeutic approach combines the energy-oriented insights of Alexander Lowen with the symbolic orientation of Carl Jung. He uses a combination of self-expression through movement, play, sandtray and art materials in a safe, contained environment to help free children from the rage, fear and grief, which have imprisoned their spirits.

Reading *If You Turned into a Monster* one is reminded of D.W. Winnicott's claim that children, in the right therapeutic environment, can often make giant steps toward healing and wholeness in a relatively short time. However, it is rare to find a therapist who has the sensitivity and skill to create a "temenos" – a safe and sacred psychological space – in which children feel free to allow their monsters into the room, express their forbidden feelings, and release the emotions they have heretofore locked within their bodies. Dennis McCarthy clearly has this gift and rapport with children. He leads us on a moving journey into their inner world and the symbols that convey their fears and their aliveness. We emerge closer to ourselves and wiser as parents, teachers and therapists.

*Richmond K. Greene,*
*Jungian Analyst, New York City*

# A Note on the Text

All names in the cases presented in the text have changed, as well as any information that would render them recognizable. But I have worked with thousands of children in my 30-plus years of practice, many with similar symptoms and family/life situations. I have not altered any of the relevant details of the child's play however.

# Introduction

I am in my childhood home, and in the next room is a huge, monstrous thing. I know it is a primeval force, something older and larger and deeper than anything I have ever imagined before. I can't see it because the door is closed, but I can sense it and I am terrified. Then I discover that a side door is open and I see that I can leave without encountering the monster. I start to do so when I suddenly realize that this monstrous "thing" is somehow a part of me. I can't really escape from it. I pause in the doorway wondering what to do.

I had the above dream at the age of 18 and it really shook me up. The idea, expressed within the dream, that this monstrous thing in my house was a part of me, and inescapable as a result, changed the direction of my life. It was a first glimpse into my own psyche, a first hint at how little I knew myself. And yet this awkward first step helped me to begin a journey towards *me*. Although I had been aware of a deep longing inside of myself throughout my growing up, I hadn't yet begun to understand what was wrong. The dream told me, albeit in symbolic form. I had dealt with the overwhelming loss and pain of my early years by separating myself from my feelings, and my body also as a result. This is something all children do in the face of trauma, and to some extent as a result of the simple process of adapting to the norms of the world they live in, of both family and culture.

The disconnected feelings of grief, rage and fear from my childhood as well as parts of my own vitality, had become like something alien and menacing within my unconscious. In the dream they seemed "anti-me" rather than of me. They had become a monster. Little did I know at the time of this dream that this monster and my efforts at reconciling it would also be my salvation. I would come to use them to envision a method of working with children that was monster friendly, a method that looked and listened for this huge, primeval being that all of us contain, trying to make room for it in each child I worked with.

At the time I had this dream I had begun to study dance, and I'm certain that the act of moving my body had the effect of stirring things up on a deep level within me. Through movement I began the process of self-discovery, and by lifting my arms and bending and leaping in the dance I began to reconnect to my own aliveness, began to open the door to the monster, though on a largely unconscious level at first. For the monster was my own aliveness, cut off but still living in me albeit as something dreaded. Thus began a journey of study and personal exploration that continues to this day.

Shortly after dreaming that dream I saw a film entitled *Looking For Me* that showed the work of a dance therapist named Janet Adler. Janet had developed a movement-based technique in working with autistic children that she called *synchrony*, which was inspired by the work of Carl Jung. She had discovered that by moving in synchrony (that literally means "in the same time as") with these children and by using their own movement reper-toire as language, however limited, they would slowly but surely begin to move with her and relate to her. This amazing film captures this process of emerging and reconnecting to the other and to the self through movement, the child's primary language.

Like many others who saw this film, I identified with the child as well as the therapist. I longed to be found, to be drawn out of myself and yet deeper into myself at the same time. I was in fact "looking for me". I decided to train as a dance therapist, which I went on to do. Through this non-verbal approach I found that simple movements when explored or repeated could lead to memories, emotions and imagery that have transformative powers.

I then discovered the work of Alexander Lowen and Wilhelm Reich, which helped me begin to understand *the monster* on a deeper, energetic level. Both of these psychiatrists used chronic muscular tensions as a point of entry into the psyche. In releasing the blocks that caused the tensions by using manual pressure and/or physical exercises which elicited a strong emotional release, they attempted to help the person reunite with parts of themselves that they had been cut off from. In the supervision that I received from Dr. Lowen his main interest in the children I presented to him was how they moved and how they didn't move. By this he wasn't simply speaking of their gross motor movements but the way the children moved within themselves as well, and how their energy flowed. As simplistic as this may seem, it became for me a most powerful diagnostic tool as well as an effective means of working with a child towards change. It has informed all the many tech-niques I have developed or expanded in my work.

Studying and engaging in Jungian analysis gave me a deeper under-standing of the monster from an imaginal perspective. The idea that an image, whether in a dream, a sand scene or any play configuration, could contain energy was a real awakening. In Lowen's work, energy was accessed directly through body movement. In the Jungian approach it was possible to access it via dreams and active imagining when awake. Rather than seeing my monster as simply pure instinct or buried rage, I began to see it in a new light, using it as a doorway into a world of other images. My monster dream did after all catapult me into action in my life, pushing me to begin the quest for myself. My monster was a doorway and provided the initial energy to move through it.

As a doorway, this monster led to a labyrinth which I am still wandering in, continuing to pick up threads and following them as they lead me deeper in rather than out. I know now that the treasure that lies therein is simply the experience of being in it, the self-awareness that this wandering fosters. Through my work with children and adults and my own self-exploration I keep asking questions and continue to be awed by the depth of our collective human experience and the myriad riches that even the most troubling of childhoods can present to us if we are willing to engage on a non-verbal level.

For the most profound of our experiences and our insights come without words. They are unspeakable except as image or pure feeling. They may arise in the pictorial images of dreams or play configurations. They may manifest in artwork or daydreams or the semi-conscious musings of the active imagi-nation. They may surface when we move without censoring it. They might use words if we speak in poetry or uncensored prose, but they are unspeak-able in the traditional sense.

When I began to work with children, I discovered that it was possible to engage them very rapidly in a meaningful and productive form of self-expression, by going with their impulses rather than imposing mine, and by assuming that they would speak more therapeutically and more satisfyingly if they were allowed and even encouraged to do so in non-verbal ways.

I found it was possible to be in-synch with a child in a variety of play activities, which gave them the potential to be deeply therapeutic because of this shared primary language. Because I had a goal and a direction I was working towards yet worked within a spontaneous child-centered format, children felt the safety of an adult in control and containing them, yet the freedom to lead me, to dictate the details of how and what we would express.

The techniques I have used and this paradoxical approach have been especially effective in working with very difficult children: children who were mute, hyperactive, oppositional, neurologically impaired, regressed or unreachable through conventional means. Just as in my own life I needed to make peace with the monster of my dream, reclaiming those parts of myself which it signified, so too these children needed the opportunity to work through their problems, not by rising above them but by using their symptoms or negative behavior to reach a level of health where these were no longer needed. In doing so they became amenable to other forms of behavior and expression naturally, with their integrity intact.

Many years ago a boy came from a great distance to see me each week and almost never spoke to me. He made several monster drawings and played intensely in the sand, however, and his symptoms rapidly disappeared. He looked and acted more self-possessed and his day-to-day life was going very well. I asked him one day why he enjoyed coming to see me so much. He thought about it briefly and said simply "I can really talk to you." I was surprised, as he had rarely spoken to me. When I mentioned this he looked at me with great disbelief. He had been busily making an elaborate scene in the sand at the time. He simply nodded with his head towards the sand in amazement, as if to say "This is how I talk, silly." And that was that.

My work with children evolved into a multifaceted approach, combining movement, sandplay, drama, clay and various art materials, but always with a central sense of how the child moved, and always aware that the most important things that might be said would be said without words. I discovered that the monster was a frequent theme for them also. All of them had already started to close doors on parts of themselves and begun to view these now alien parts as monsters to be feared rather than as necessary and even wonderful parts of themselves.

Children's spiritedness is the root of their being. This basic spirit, this vital energy, not only is how the self expresses itself, but it is the self.

Nowhere is it so vibrant as in young children. It literally leaps up in them. But eventually in most children it is thwarted to some degree, if not destroyed altogether. In the children whom I work with the suppression of this spirit and energy has caused enough problems that the adult world has taken notice. Freeing up this thwarted energy is the basis of the therapy described within these pages, and must be how we work with children if we are to bring about a deep level of transformation, rather than simply make superficial changes.

Looking at my monster dream in light of this I can see that my own energy was so tied up in suppressing the monster, in keeping the door closed, that there was little available for other life-affirming purposes. How to open the unopened door? How to encounter the beast that stands therein? In the therapy described in the following pages, the monster is a central theme used to access this life-essential energy that has transformative power.

My purpose in writing this book is to share with parents, teachers, therapists and adults in general an approach to reinstating a sense of wholeness in the child that is body-centered. This approach utilizes the imagination in a body-centered format. Imagination and the body together are how children grow and heal. I hope that looking at this approach and the many children described in these pages who have helped me to better define it may offer also a deeper sense of what it is to be a child and therefore what it is to be human.

I have come to believe that all the myriad problems which children struggle with amount to the same problem: how to live with the bigness of life that exists both within us and around us. Children live closer to this bigness, with less interference and less protection from its intensity. External events such as trauma or parental mistakes can of course affect further our ability to negotiate this bigness. Neurological problems, so common these days, can also make the regulation of this much more challenging, but our own bigness remains for me the central issue.

Parents play a peripheral role in the following pages, although they play a central one in the life of their children and the ontology of their problems. I have chosen to focus mainly on the child and on the phenomenon of childhood in general. I believe this has been sorely lacking in the literature that exists. Rarely is the child as an individual allowed to speak on his or her own largely non-verbal terms, but rather they are usually spoken about primarily in terms of pathology or skewed family systems. There are two seriously flawed implications in this approach.

Children are of course profoundly affected by the families they are a part of, but to be human is a difficult thing for all of us. Even a relatively healthy family produces children who may struggle enormously, as people have always done, with the question of "Who am I?" Second, children's symptoms often contain within them great things, such as thwarted but potentially life-affirming energies, images such as that of my dream monster that can lead us towards ourselves. Symptoms often contain the key to open the doorway to self-exploration as well as the doorway itself. This journey, taken out of necessity, may foster great things, especially if it is a creative journey. To focus on pathology misses all of this and as a result misses who the child really is. Because the key exists in the child and not in their family system, the very means of unlocking the door will be missed.

Children are usually looked at and listened to in a detached and overly intellectualized manner by the many adults who attempt to help them. But to know and help the child we must speak their language or at least know they are speaking it. We must also see their underlying health, however thwarted, for it is this health that will be the guide. I do work with parents to varying degrees, encouraging them to better understand themselves as well as their children, along with helping them make room for the health that will hopefully be fostered by the play therapy process.

But I want the child to take center stage in these pages, and in doing so teach us not simply about childhood problems, of which we know something, but about health and vibrancy, which although our birthright remain elusive.

Chapter 1

# "If You Turned into a Monster"

"Draw a picture of what you would look like if you turned into a monster," I tell the seven-year-old sitting stiffly before me. It is our first session together so we are both feeling a bit awkward. She looks wide-eyed with disbelief at my request. Her parents have most likely told her that she is coming to talk to me about her problems. I try again. "Imagine you have drunk a magic potion and your body is changing into that of a monster. Really try and imagine that it's happening to you. Then draw what you look like." She realizes I am quite serious and with that the little girl smiles and proceeds to draw a spectacular beast with bulging eyes, an enormous mouth and two huge fangs dripping with blood. When she finishes she is obviously quite pleased with the outcome. "Does it have a name?" I inquire. Without any hesitation she christens it "Mouth." "And what does your monster do that makes it so monstrous?" I ask. Again, without hesitation and even with a touch of confidence she exclaims, "It eats everyone."

When I first meet a child with whom I am going to be working therapeutically, I usually ask the child to draw himself or herself as a monster. I do so for a variety of reasons. Monsters are after all our first creative acts as humans. From early on we dream them and imagine them. They dwell under our beds or behind our bedroom doors. They peek in through our windows. They are often right on the edge of our developing consciousness, part instinctual urge and part deity. We wake our parents in the middle of the night because of them, and our parents try ineffectually to dispel them by saying things like "There's no such thing as monsters" or "It was just a dream." But all their reassurances and dismissals are to no avail, for as young children we know that these first creative acts of ours, no matter how much we dislike them, do exist and are "ours." They belong to us and somehow they are us. If only our parents would express an interest in these beasts, as well as trying to comfort us. If only they asked "What did it look like tonight?" their children would not feel so alone with the power that these monsters personify. But we as parents have lost direct access to our own monsters. We too fear these beasts. We doubt the truth of our dreams.

These first creative acts of ours are a mixture of instincts, emotion and also an early experience of deity. They are the child's efforts at negotiating the bigness of life, both within themselves and around them, in all its ramifications. Children almost always respond to my request with disbelief and then relief. Even the more timid of children such as the above child are eager to speak through this monstrous form. They know this, more than they consciously know themselves.

Children come to therapy with monstrous feelings – monstrous grief, monstrous rage, monstrous longing – to name a few. These feelings are unacceptable, unfaceable, and unmanageable to themselves, as well as to the world around them. The invitation to draw themselves as a monster is an immediate acknowledgment of these feelings as fact, and an acceptance of their existence and legitimacy. Children receive this communication on an intuitive level, the primary level on which deep communication takes place with children. I also, in a sense, form a potential allegiance with this monster, symbol and composite of so much. By giving it permission to exist as a part of our relationship, I immediately dissipate some of the negative power that it possesses.

Many things begin to happen as a result of this allegiance. The drawing itself, what it actually expresses and, even more important, how the child experiences it, can point the way towards health. The above child's monster, with its overemphasized fanged mouth, could be seen to indicate a need and a desire to sink one's teeth into life. It would suggest that a great deal of anger would be released along the way. The ease with which she drew it tells me that beneath her shy exterior she is a real dynamo. Perhaps it is this very thwarted dynamism that has turned into the list of symptoms she has come to therapy with. The act of expressing this thwarted energy via such a drawing is a significant step in the process of redirecting it. Part of the child's self, which has been repressed or never developed, can begin to emerge and evolve simply by making the statement which the drawing makes, that is, "This is me," or "This is how I feel."

The variety of monster drawings presented to me is astounding, from the ridiculous to the sublime, but almost all with an edge of humor. Even the most violent "self" monster drawings have a humorous twist. I think this says much about our potential as humans, that this paradoxical ability to embrace all aspects of the human experience in one form is still present in young children. When do we lose this I wonder?

One of the first children I ever worked with over 30 years ago brought me a book of Eskimo tales as a gift. The first story in the book was called "The Giant Bear." The book has long since disappeared from my collection and I have been unable to find the story reprinted elsewhere. Yet it is quite vivid in my mind.

> Once a giant bear was ravaging the countryside, eating everyone it came upon. The people of the area were terrified, but one young boy set out to find the bear. Everywhere he went in his search for the giant bear people told him, "Are you crazy? Run for your life!" Yet he continued on his way and eventually came upon the bear. He rushed up to it and allowed himself to be eaten. The monster swallowed him in one gulp. Once inside the bear's belly, the boy took out his knife. He carved a door in the bear's stomach and leapt out, killing the bear, of course. Then he freed all those who had been eaten and called everyone together to help him butcher the bear. And there was bear meat for many months to come. That's the way it goes; monster one minute and food the next.

Our basic response to a story such as this is on a gut level. We *feel* what it means. And it is precisely on this gut, feeling level that psychotherapy with children takes place. It is from here that the child speaks and it's from the same place in ourselves that we must listen. We rarely need to analyze or interpret. In fact, to do so often interferes with the process that is taking place.

It is the use of metaphor and allegory that makes stories such as this so profound, and it is this same metaphoric language which children speak in every play configuration they make, be it drawings, clay figures, sandplay or stories. Our task is not to translate but to accept it as it is. Its richness exists in its allusion to, its insinuation.

The huge mouth monster created by the seven-year-old of herself is experienced as "of her self." Thereby the regenerative power the monster possesses is also experienced as "of the self."

Literature abounds with examples of transformation involving monsters. In Maurice Sendak's *Where the Wild Things Are*, the child Max, after being punished by his mother for being too wild, travels in his imagination to a land of monsters where he is king. He roars and gnashes his teeth with them until he has vented his frustration. Then he sails back home, his integrity intact (Sendak 1963).

In C.S. Lewis's *Voyage of the Dawntreader*, there is a selfish, unloved, and unlovable child named Eustace, who at one point puts on a magic bracelet and is transformed into a dragon. In this monstrous state he experiences how much like a monster he really is. Eventually he is healed, the dragon skin and the armor of his defenses peeled off, layer by layer. In the end he appears in his original state, vulnerable but human (Lewis 1988).

In the classic French fairy tale "Beauty and the Beast" a prince has been enchanted and changed into a hideous beast. The character Beauty eventually breaks the spell by loving him despite his beastliness, by recognizing the deeper beauty within him. The beast is transformed only by a total acceptance of it (Perrault 1961). The main characters in all of these stories are transformed too by their encounters with the beasts. They become more mature and more human.

These stories, and many others like them, move us because they describe a transformation in which what is vital in the person is affirmed, freed or reborn. We also relate to them, especially the child or the child in us, because somehow we know that transformation only happens by accepting the monster.

In working with children we must help provoke this type of transformation in what is a paradoxical manner. The therapist hands out the magic bracelet and then helps peel off the skin. He shows the child where the Giant Bear is and then helps with the butchering. He accompanies the monsters dancing in the land of the wild things and then pushes the child's boat off for home. He makes the realm of the Beast less terrifying, so that the child can make peace with the part of himself or herself that dwells there. Through a combination of humor and great seriousness he plays the role of guide and assistant, yet steps out of the way quickly so as not to interfere with the forces of play.

For the most part, the monsters that children draw in therapy have nothing in common with the monsters with which television and movies bombard us. Adults whose aim, aside from making money, is to horrify us, create these monsters. That these monsters are compelling to children has to do with the feelings of horror they evoke. In a lecture by Alexander Lowen entitled "Horror: The Face of Unreality" he asserts:

> I have often wondered why children are fascinated by horror movies.
> ... I have thought that it represented their need to overcome the sense
> of horror enough to be able to function in a world that contained much
> horror. But the introduction of horror via movies does not help us cope
> with horror. It blinds us to horror by making us assume that it is a
> natural part of life. We learn to accept the horror, not reject it, and we
> become victims of horror. (Lowen 1972, p.1)

The media uses monstrous images to create numbness and disassociation. It hooks us with its horrific images that serve no therapeutic value, in fact quite the opposite. This aspect is not usually present in the monsters that children draw for me. The media, by bombarding children with adult-generated images of horror, does real damage to the child's developing psyche. I find that nowadays I sometimes have to help children reach into themselves through a layer of mechanized and horror-induced numbness. But rather quickly in most cases the real monsters emerge, the ancient ones! These ancient ones arise from deep within and far from disconnecting us from ourselves they open doors or keep a pathway open to a deeper connection.

With most children, the spontaneous monsters which they create literally out of themselves are life affirming. Their grotesqueness, and any violence they describe, has potentially a healing function. The point is not to horrify but to rectify, to change a situation that is negatively energized, and that threatens the child's integrity. We may begin to understand this transformative process better by looking at one child's monsters in particular.

## The key to the heart

Eli was a six-year-old brought for therapy with a long list of symptoms. These included thumb sucking, wetting and soiling his pants, self-stimulation and social withdrawal. Due to this latter, Eli had no friends. He got along well with adults and possessed a rather adult vocabulary, despite all the infantile symptoms. This dichotomy between his adult-like demeanor and his infant-like symptoms was significant.

Some of the symptoms from infancy had only partially disappeared, at which point they were normal behaviors. Still others were part of an overall regression, triggered by the hospitalization of Eli's father for severe alcoholism. His father had been battling alcoholism unsuccessfully for years, and had entered rehabilitation programs periodically only to fail each time. Eli's father was like a child himself, perhaps explaining Eli's need to act grown-up.

Eli's mother, though a more stable and mature individual, felt overwhelmed by the responsibility of being the sole breadwinner and parent. She also felt a sense of guilt and hopelessness about her weak husband, rather than anger, which would have been more appropriate and empowering, but "not nice." Eli, for both his parents' sakes and with them as role models, was overly obedient and helpful. Yet his body was expressing his deeper feelings and his level of functioning was deteriorating rapidly.

At our first meeting Eli entered the play space eager to please me, yet also eager to play. His body was very small for his age and his head was disproportionately large. He looked very sad and worried, with the weight of the world on his tiny shoulders. Eli sat down and drew a monster at my request. The monster he drew was actually a large key with human features. It had no name and no attributes. After exploring, with satisfaction, the other possibilities in the play setting, he came back to the drawing and added a small heart next to the key. "It's the key to the heart," he said simply. "Take care of it!" (Figure 1.1).

*Figure 1.1 The "key to the heart" monster*

After handing me the heart-key monster drawing, Eli used my office bathroom. This was the first time he had used a toilet rather than his pants in many weeks. As is often the case, there was a direct body connection in his imaginal play. Eli was saying something so important in handing me his monster, yet neither of us needed to know exactly what was being said. What was important is that it *was*.

In subsequent sessions, Eli began each time with a monster drawing, or sometimes he leapt up in the middle of his play and spontaneously began to draw a monster. These monsters were all very alive. Huge, slithering, coiling snake-like creatures, they covered the paper and eventually my walls. Some had several heads and all were exploding with energy. They all had elaborate names. Many of them evolved or metamorphosed while he was drawing them, and the best way to describe the series was "matter transforming itself." This changing, volatile energy was actually palpable in the room as Eli worked on his drawings (Figure 1.2).

*Figure 1.2 Eli's drawings: matter transforming itself*

The remainder of each session entailed his embodying and using this newly formed energy in a variety of ways. Fighting with me with foam "encounter bats" was a means of experiencing and directing his emerging aggression at someone who could accept it and yet give it limits. Building huge towers out of blocks and smashing them down gave vent to both the creative and destructive aspects of this aggression. As is often the case with children like Eli, he began by being concerned with making these towers correctly. This evolved into his destroying them and then eventually he came back to creating them for their own sake. These later block assemblages were much more interesting and dynamic.

Most of Eli's symptoms disappeared very quickly as the raw energy, expressed by his monsters, went through its various representations. The thwarted, inner-directed aggression, which had manifested itself in regressive symptoms, became outer-directed. As his monsters changed so did he and vice versa.

Eli began to experiment with asserting himself socially, albeit awkwardly at first. His first forays at socializing often ended in fistfights, but both his mother and his teacher were able, with guidance, to accept this new behavior, seeing it as a step towards health. As Eli embodied the energy and power that his monsters described, he became able to express his feelings, especially those surrounding his father's illness. Although Eli's father didn't change, Eli was able to do so and actually inspired his mother to do so as well. In accepting Eli's need to express and assert himself she came to accept this need in herself as well.

As Eli became truly more childlike, his infantile symptoms disappeared and he seemed less like a little adult. His performance in school improved not only socially but academically as well. Although Eli was exceptionally bright, he had been unable to manifest this in school. He was too withdrawn and preoccupied. But as his aggression emerged in his play sessions, this changed. The connection between the expression of "negativity" and knowledge is the key here. In his book *Pleasure*, Alexander Lowen makes this connection quite clear:

> To what extent is the negative an essential ingredient of knowledge? Knowledge is a function of discrimination. To know what A is, it must be distinguished from all that is not A. Knowledge arises from the recognition of differences. The first difference that an organism can recognize is that between what feels good to the body or pleasurable and what feels painful. (Lowen 1970, p.155)

When Eli handed me "the key to the heart" in our first visit he was demanding a level of responsibility, maturity and care from me that his own father had been unable to manage. Eli had never made demands of his father, nor had his mother for that matter. His father was too sick, too weak, and too helpless. By being able to make a demand of an adult male, Eli immediately took a giant step forward. I believe his immediate use of the bathroom after doing so was a result of being able to make the demand.

In Erik Erikson's book *Toys and Reasons* he describes three types of play which children use in therapy:

> If we acknowledge in certain play configurations the working through of some traumatic experience, we also note that the very factor of playfulness transforms them into acts of renewal. If some such events seem to be governed by the need to communicate, or even to confess something, the element of playfulness adds the joy of self-expression. And if the play so obviously helps the exercise of growing faculties, it does so with inventiveness and abandon. (Erikson 1977, p.42)

To these three types of play – traumatic, cathartic and integrative – that Erikson is describing, I would add a fourth one – explorative. The act of exploring the possibilities for self-expression, release and integration in and of itself can greatly assist transformation. Many children spend much of their therapy in this exploratory stage.

Eli made use of all of these types of play, as do most children. As he became able to embody the power and aliveness that his monsters represented, he found the strength and courage to go forward in his life.

## The shadow

The monstrous imaginings seen thus far resemble the Jungian concept of the *shadow*. The term has various meanings. On the one hand it is seen to be those qualities or characteristics that the civilizing process demands that we negate. Rather than disappear, they live on in our unconscious.

Aside from the demands of society, families too require that children give up aspects of themselves in order to fit within a particular family system. In one family it might be aggression or self-assertion, and in another tenderness or vulnerability. Many families tolerate very little that is genuine to the child. But the refused and unacceptable characteristics do not go away. They only collect in the dark corners of our personality. When they have hidden long enough they take on a life of their own – the shadow life. The shadow is that which has not entered adequately into consciousness. It is the despised quarter of our being. The shadow gone autonomous is a terrible monster in our psychic house (Johnson 1991).

If we look at the children described thus far, it is possible to see aspects of their developing shadow side in the monsters they created. Children's negative feelings, so understandable yet so intolerable to them without the support and acceptance of someone else, still continue to live on in them with great determination.

The little girl in the opening paragraph did come to embody the biting power that her first monster expressed. If she had not done so, if it had remained unconscious, those blood-dripping fangs might have sunk themselves into her own psyche and also into those she was close to.

Eli's passive exterior belied the enormous aggression bubbling away beneath the surface. His "key" monster with its accompanying heart suggests that his heart was already becoming locked up tight. Had it remained so he may have grown into an isolated young man, probably turning to drink as his father had done. His shadow, containing so much aggressive power, would have taken its toll on him and anyone he might try to be close with. The capacity to love and the capacity to aggress are closely linked. To aggress, after all, means "to move towards."

We all possess a shadow side. How familiar we are with it, how much energy we have reclaimed from it, depends on how much work we have done on ourselves, how much we have struggled to become conscious. This aspect, so evasive and difficult to accept, is essential in order to become whole: "The shadow is a tight passage, a narrow door, whose painful constriction no one is spared who goes down to the deep well" (Jung 1959, p.21).

Children are unique in their capacity to encounter their monsters and their developing shadow in a spirit of playfulness and even with great humor. This capacity is due in part to the symbolic nature of their play.

## Acknowledgment

Parts of this chapter were previously published in an article by Dennis McCarthy (1977), "If You Turned into a Monster," *Bioenergetic Analysis 8*, 1, pp.99–105.

# Chapter 2

# Symbols and Symbolic Play

The journey to the "deep well" is synonymous with the process of "individu-ation," Jung's term for self-actualization. It is the process "by which a person becomes a separate, indivisible unity or whole" (Jung 1959, p.251). It is a journey we begin from the moment we are born, and it is possible to look at all dreams, all creative imaginings that occur, especially within the context of therapy, as the efforts of our deeper self to help us actualize this journey, as well as an expression of the enormous resistance most of us have to it. This journey is both embarked upon and realized in part through the formation and use of symbols.

All language, in its origin and essence, is simply a system of signs or symbols that denote real occurrences or their echo in the human soul. As adults we are always attempting to express the largely unspeakable experi-ence of being alive and all that this entails by using language. But when the language used is not convoluted through words or a conscious, intentional thought but is offered more directly as it springs from the imagination, it comes much closer to translating life, to connecting us to others and to ourselves. Children speak in the immediate language of the body and the imagination, their symbols being a composite of the two – body and mind.

In Anthony Steven's book *Archetypes* he formulates a definition of the word symbol which I find the most meaningful. Taken from the ancient Greek, the word symbol means "a token of identification," a means by which members of a tribe could verify their relatedness. Two members upon meeting could compare their "symbols," which might be a bone or a coin broken in half. Its fit would confirm their identity by forming a whole, a "gestalt" (Stevens 1983). The symbols we produce then in sandplay or monster drawings, in dreams or any active imagination technique, are all efforts to find a way of fitting and belonging both to our deeper and higher selves and to the great human tribe and even to the cosmos.

The more common definition of the word symbol is something that represents something else, especially a material object used to represent something invisible. Symbols allude to things that are deeper and beyond words, which are often of the utmost importance.

When the child makes a drawing, tells a story, or makes a scene in the sandbox, we have before us in symbolic form the closest glimpse possible of the human psyche. They not only become what they create, they *are* this with no clear delineation. When in the presence of a sand scene, for example, it feels, in an almost shamanistic manner, that the child's psyche is actually to some extent "in the sand." This is especially so when the play is *charged*, that is, when there is a palpable sense of aliveness in the play configuration. In these numinous moments there is no separation between the child and their imaginings. Body and psyche are one and equally present in the activity. Because of this these charged moments can allow for remarkable transformation. The child may stand up from the sandbox after such an experience and really be reorganized or renewed. I hope to offer many examples of this in the coming pages.

"These symbols speak for the energy-laden pictures of the innate potentials of the child which when manifest always influence the child's development" (Kalff 1980, p.29). In Dora Kalff's classic book *Sand Play*, she offers two key aspects of children's symbols that explain their power. They are pictorial images of wholeness or the path to wholeness and they are energy-laden. The energy within a symbol becomes available to the child once it is manifest. Accessing the symbol accesses the energy, and the accessed energy has the potential to further express itself in even more alive images. Thus the idea of symbol to energy keeps on going to symbol again, and on and on.

There are symbols and then there are *symbols*. The miniature figures selected by a therapist for his or her office are not really symbols in and of themselves. They are simply miniature figures that have the potential to help children better articulate and explore themselves. Their becoming a symbol, a vehicle of transformation, depends on what happens inside the child as they sit there. A figure of a horse or a herd of horses may be used by a little girl as she struggles to find her power, her true voice. The raw energy of the horses charging through the sand becomes a symbol of what is trying to surface within her and also a catalyst for it. But a moment before, the horse was just a plastic figure on a shelf. Its sudden relevance is based not on the object itself but rather on the child, how she associates with it, what her body does with it, and how meaningfully it expresses and even fosters the great upsurge within her that we call growth.

Speaking in symbols ameliorates the raw power of what is being said, serving like a surge breaker or filter. The child can say through symbols things that are unspeakable in any other form. Speaking about the unspeakable is the essence of therapeutic work. What I mean by the unspeakable is not simply negative experiences and the emotions they result in; it is also the great joy of being alive or the discovery of new parts to ourselves, both of which need to be experienced and often expressed in the play therapy process to help the child affirm the experience. How could one put into words the raw intensity of horses rushing? How could Eli say in words alone what the "key to the heart" represents to him? Children who can't speak in symbols are often unable to regulate life's intensity as a result. They are also unable to speak about the really important things. One of the first tasks with such children is to help them learn to speak in symbols.

The most exciting symbols are the ones that children create out of themselves. These are exalted *symbols*, the ones that make us quake with awe when we are in the presence of them. In creation myths from all over the world, the key element in many of them is the creation of something or even everything out of nothing, or out of chaos. The Pelasgian Creation myth from neolithic Greece describes how Eurynome, the mother of all things, takes the wind and rubs it between her hands, turning it into a great serpent. She couples with this serpent and out of this union she gives birth to everything: people, trees, flowers, rivers, etc. But it begins with nothing but a longing for more than what is. When Eurynome takes the wind and rubs it between her hands she is giving form to her longing, and the great snake Ophioussa emerges (Graves 1983).

Children too have the ability to make big things out of seemingly nothing. The little girl who drew her big fanged mouth monster did so out of seemingly nothing. Sitting there before me timid and fearful, yet also longing like Eurynome to give more solid form to her life, she was able with a little encouragement to suddenly produce an image of power that still sits on my wall inspiring other children at least 20 years later. This is true transformation rather than simple change. It is a fundamental shift in form, a revolution within.

Eli, described in Chapter 1, produced the symbol of the key within the first few minutes of our initial session. By the end of the session he was able to entrust this symbol to me, "the key to the heart" as he described it. In doing so his regressive symptoms stopped. Why? I have only my own associations to the image and my experience of the child to go by, but I see the symbol of the key as a symbol of movement, of opening or closing, of possibilities. In producing this symbol and entrusting it to me, Eli took a big step forward towards life, that is, he aggressed. The deeper isolation and thwarted aggression and the underlying feelings of grief and rage were worked through more gradually. The energy to do so was accessed in part through the ever-evolving monsters he drew each session, symbols which facilitated this change.

By creating the symbol of the key and entrusting it to me, Eli was verifying that our relationship fitted. He was also asserting his own identity. Eli's key symbol was both mysterious and powerful, a type of symbol which Jung would have described as "numinous," having an elevated quality or charge to it. For me, numinous symbols like Eli's key are similar to milestones in a child's growth, such as their first step or first words. As the child accomplishes this first step, those who witness it feel a great sense of awe and delight. When the child creates a symbol that is numinous in the course of therapy, it is as if a psychic first step has been mastered, a first word uttered. They are giving form to something that is archetypal and yet deeply personal. They are able to know something through it that is central to whom they are both personally and collectively.

Recently a young girl, Sarah, began therapy in the midst of a family crisis. Her father was dying of Aids. Not only did she have to deal with his imminent death, but she had to cope with the circumstances of his illness as well. He had contracted the virus through frequent sexual activity that he knew ran the risk of exposing himself to the virus. This had been going on for many years and thus he had run the risk of exposing his wife and children to the virus also.

The conflicting feelings of rage, grief, and shock were overwhelming to Sarah's mother, let alone herself. Although Sarah described herself in our visit as feeling numb, her face was full of anger and hurt. It was obvious that because of her father's ill health it would be difficult for her to vent her angry feelings at him or even about him. Yet it was imperative that she, and her mother also, do so in order for the possibility of forgiveness to occur.

In one of her first visits Sarah was able to express this anger through clay. She created a large monster out of clay and I did likewise. Then our monsters did battle. At first, although enjoying the experience, she was holding back until I suggested that she picture my monster as someone or something in particular which she was angry at.

This immediately increased the amount of energy she put into the battle. She pulverized my monster again and again and again. Clay is a perfect material for this type of angry discharge. Sarah's rage eventually gave way to tears and she spoke about the fears and hopelessness she felt in the shadow of her father's horrible illness. She had to keep all these feelings to herself. She feared, and rightfully so, that if her peers knew of her father's illness she would be ostracized at school.

As Sarah talked she began to change her own monster. Gradually she transformed it into a multi-tiered fountain. She did so unconsciously and was very surprised at the outcome. She held her fountain aloft, quite pleased and moved by it. She took it home with her that day and it sat by her bedside throughout the ensuing months during which her father died.

The fountain, which she created out of her angry discharge, gave her the courage and strength to face this loss. The fountain is a symbol of both hope and renewal. Both she and her mother, through her own therapy, were able to go beyond their anger and make peace with him before he died. He died with them at his side, a deep healing having occurred.

Yet another child who was afflicted with a potentially terminal illness began one day, after many weeks of angry discharge, to create a pair of wings. This happened very suddenly, in the same way that Sarah's fountain emerged out of anger. They were a surprise to both of us. But he was unusually insistent about it. At first I suspected that he was making a joke. He was a very cynical child at times and often spoke of things with sarcastic humor that another child might do with reverence. But it seemed that he really wanted to make wings. They were made out of paper and he let me help him cut them out and also help him color in each rainbow-hued feather. He worked on these wings in each session for several weeks in total silence. When they were done he had me put them away. He never spoke about them while he made them or afterwards. He didn't need to. For this child who faced likely death to make wings clearly helped him in some deep way. Whatever they meant for him was bigger than words or any meaning I might ascribe to them. They simply were.

These symbols looked at thus far were all made out of the child rather than selected by me. They weren't figures on my shelves, although I have thousands of these that do get used. But rather these images emerged out of the child without a conscious intention. The child seemed to give birth to them in the moment of their inception and they also seem to arise from some deep and profoundly human source. When the child is able to manifest hope or renewal in symbolic form it is the beginning or resumption of healthy ego development. This symbol is always a sign of inner order, which allows growth to resume.

## Roles of the therapist

The therapist's roles in this symbol-making, energy-accessing process are that of the *witness*, the *container*, the *instigator* and the *visionary*. Each is a pivotal component in facilitating the process. Each is required to a lesser or greater extent depending on the child. They may overlap and happen simultaneously. Often we are witnessing, containing and provoking all at the same time, with a vision of where we are hoping to go as well, yet it is helpful to look at these roles as if separate. First is that of the witness. Whether this witnessing is passive or interactive, it is an essential part of the transformative process. Because emotions always seek an object, the underlying emotions in symbolic play need the presence of an empathetic person who sees them. As witness we are not necessarily saying anything. We are simply "the other" and as such we concretize what occurs. We ground it for the child by being a witness to it. Sometimes it is necessary to be an active witness, participating in and even provoking what occurs. In my own approach, I offer myself as the recipient or sounding board for the aggression that often erupts in this process. Sometimes I provoke or instigate the symbol-making process, such as in encouraging children to draw themselves as monsters. But usually the child will dictate how active a role the witnessing therapist will play.

## Active witnessing

James, aged seven, was referred for therapy by his pediatrician due to the frequent bowel and bladder "accidents" he was having. These happened only in the presence of his mother, an unemployed nurse who was obsessively concerned with James's health.

His parents had divorced when he was very young, and James saw his father on weekends. His father was furious at the infantilizing behavior of his ex-wife towards their son. Unfortunately, he directed this fury towards James when he saw him, acting disappointed in him, which created a roadblock to his natural maturation. This undermined the very relationship with his father that James so desperately needed. In reaction to her ex-husband's anger, James's mother would coddle her son all the more.

This tendency to take opposite approaches from each other can create a power struggle that escalates the extremes of both sides. Even when the approach is motivated by good intentions, it winds up hurting the child, but

when it is caused, as in the case of James's mother, by a parent's own unresolved needs the effect can be devastating. In my initial meeting with James's
mother I asked her what might happen if she focused less on James's health.
She responded that she suspected she would become very depressed. As
James became healthy via his therapeutic process, his mother did become
depressed and went into therapy herself.

James gave the physical impression in our first meeting of a very large
infant. His body still had the pudgy, amorphous quality associated with
babies. He seemed as yet unformed, but there was a spark in his eyes. He
separated easily from his mother and looked quite eager to play. James began
his first visit with me by casually examining all the objects in the room.
There was a humorous and also an intentional quality to his seemingly
passive exploration of the space and its contents. He indirectly made his way
towards an empty side room that was attached to my office which had a bare
wood floor. He removed his shoes, walked into the center of the floor and
began to slip suddenly, as if he were on ice. After a great deal of slipping with
a great deal of drama, he collapsed. With enormous effort he rose to his feet,
only to collapse again. It was very funny but it also felt very important. Eventually he asked me to help him up. He allowed me to do so, very dramatically,
pulling me down with him several times before he actually let me get him on
to his feet and help him off the "ice."

During James's first two visits, he spent most of the time in the above
"slipping" ritual. In the third visit, after repeating the ritual several times, he
drew a picture of a snake. The slipping routine continued in future sessions,
as did the snake drawing. Each week he slipped less and the snake grew
longer, eventually spanning several sheets of paper the length of the room.
Then the snake's head began to grow larger. As it grew, so did the size and
number of its teeth. At the same time its body began to shrink, till eventually
it was all head and teeth with only a small tail. It thus resembled a sperm cell
with teeth.

At this point all the rituals stopped. James's remaining visits were spent
building huge towers out of blocks and conceiving complicated ways of
demolishing them. In this final phase James was like an artist, scientist and
demolition crew all rolled into one.

James had stopped using his bowels and bladder to express himself after
his very first visit. The "slipping on ice" symbol not only expressed the
problem but also contained the energy for the second symbol, the snake, to
emerge. Once the snake emerged, James actually began to look different. His
body, which at the onset of therapy had the look of a large infant, became

elongated and more defined, just like his snakes. As he reached out to let me help him up in his slipping rituals, he was also beginning to develop a group of buddies in his neighborhood. He became more aggressive and assertive as he discovered his legs, stood on his own two feet and claimed his sexual identity through the two symbols in his play. James's mother, with encouragement, became proud of the health she saw in him rather than the illness she imagined. James's father took his son's symptoms less personally and, by welcoming him as he was, encouraged him to change.

## Active containing

Another role of the therapist is that of the container. The therapist establishes the boundaries in which the process of playful transformation will occur. This is done primarily on a non-verbal level. The therapist holds the child in his awareness, which becomes a holding environment that the child can actually feel. By communicating non-verbally (and verbally if need be) that the space and relationship are strong enough and safe enough to handle whatever might emerge, the child can immediately begin the process of change. Most children will sense this and respond to it very quickly, as we see in the case of James. His examining of objects gave him time to sense the container, and check out the witness. In James's case he needed no provocation as his playful spirit provided it for him, that is, he provoked himself and me as well. When we look at how much the symbols which children work with are actually raw material of the self, it is easy to see how essential safety and containability are.

Some children take longer, needing to test the waters. Younger children, children with organic or medical problems and sexually abused children will often require more containment and take more time to trust the boundaries enough to begin to evolve. Part of healthy containing is sensing when the time is ripe.

The room itself forms a boundary or container, especially in its designation as the space within which the therapeutic relationship occurs. When the sandbox or sandtray is used, as it usually is to some extent, it adds another layer of containment. Between the room, the witnessing therapist, and the sandbox we have three layers of containment. I often think of the whole process as being like a *mandala*. The mandala, meaning "magic circle," is used in meditation to alter consciousness towards wholeness. The act of witnessing and containing the symbol-making, energy-accessing process in play therapy is also mandalic, with ultimately the same goal.

## Provocative play

One little boy announced to me one day that he was going to become a seed. He proceeded to curl up on the ground and for at least ten minutes was silent and still. I witnessed and contained this quiet process and then I became a bit concerned. Would he ever emerge from this seed form I wondered? What if he hadn't done so by the time the session ended? What would his mother say if she came in and found her son had turned into a seed but not emerged again? So out of my own impatience I finally inquired, "Would the seed like a little water to help it grow?" A much stronger voice than he had ever used before came form the curled up from saying, "If you would be quiet and leave him alone the seed will grow just fine!" So I sat, put in my place by this once very passive little boy, and after another five minutes passed he leapt up into the air with a loud "Tadah!" He had become a large tomato plant, covered with juicy fruit.

I had thought at the time that my nervous questioning of the child was simply interference, but I realized long afterwards in thinking about him that it was a provocation, or at least it was used as such by this child. He needed me to interfere so that he could push against me. His growing when he finally did had more oomph to it, his voice more self assuredness in it because he had been able to silence me. And I had backed off, making room for this newer, energetically bigger child.

Usually I am aware of my provoking children and do so when it feels needed, when the play itself is not serving that function. This provocation might take the form of introducing a new figure into a child's play that has been repetitive in a rigid, non-therapeutic sense. For example, a child may make a scene in which two armies are engaged in battle and week after week the action remains the same with no changes described. Then I might have a dragon descend into the midst, or announce that an earthquake is about to happen. Even when children reject my intrusion it adds a new variable. Even very rigid children will often incorporate this new figure into their rigid play. If the figure is non-rigid, such as a dragon or a snake, or if the event is form altering such as an earthquake, it invariably shifts the quality of the child's play. In fact, the playful yet provocative introduction of something new into rigid, repetitive play can alter not only the play but the child also, as they *are* their play.

The symbols of self looked at thus far – wings, the key, the fountain, the snake, and even the seed – are truly archetypes of wholeness, occurring as such everywhere and throughout history. They would represent the same numinous possibility when used in any story. Yet these children each felt that they had invented their symbols, out of themselves, out of their pain or stuckness. And they had. The symbol-making process is innate in the child. By giving it our awareness and containing it, and allowing the accessed energy to be expressed, it very rapidly begins to work in the service of the child's developing ego towards the resolution of inner conflicts and the rebirth of the self.

# Chapter 3

# From Symbol to Energy

## Opening scenes

Six-year-old Robert, referred to me by his teacher, entered the classroom each day like a human cyclone, instantly creating havoc. His unintentional and yet uncontrollable chaotic aggression made it impossible to teach him. The teacher spent much of her time trying to contain him, and he was both provocative with his peers and oppositional with adults.

Just as James's father had been unable to tolerate his son's passivity, Robert's father had been unable to tolerate his son's aggressiveness and also

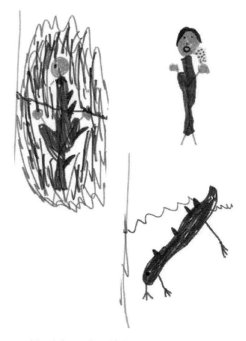

*Figure 3.1 A seven-year-old girl depicts herself changing into an underwater dragon at the onset of therapy*

unable to set limits on it. He simply rejected Robert outright, viewing him as a rival in an unhappy marriage. As a child, Robert's father had been terrorized by his mother, and escaped from her eventually by entering a seminary. He had not, however, escaped the pent-up emotions that his childhood had left him with. They contributed to his rejection of his son and to his marital difficulties. The bitterness and hurt inside sabotaged all of his efforts at closeness.

Robert's mother, on the other hand, turned to her son for the emotional closeness she could not get from her husband. An early history of sexual abuse by several adult males in her life had left her deeply scarred. She had risen above this to some extent, becoming a very successful businesswoman. Yet the inner wounds were still there.

In my initial meeting with Robert's parents, his mother assured me that Robert would never allow her to leave him alone with me but would insist upon her staying. I assured her that I would not let her stay. In this verbal interchange, which took 30 seconds, a very important transaction took place. Given her early history, I could understand how Robert's mother might not trust an adult male. That she was transferring this on to her son was also apparent. My firm insistence that it be so and success in enforcing this when Robert actually came not only set the stage but helped his mother begin a process of change.

Robert entered the play space for the first time with great bravado. He looked like a little lord, with chest puffed up and a slight swagger. At the same time I could sense an eagerness in him to play, which was the part of Robert I immediately engaged, though I knew we would have to sort out his lordliness at a later point. I invited him to make a scene in my sandbox. Robert approached the sandbox with great enthusiasm. He set to work and created the following scene in it:

> Numerous soldiers were grouped in twos, aiming their weapons at each other, throughout the sandbox at all angles. A thin ridge of sand separated each fighting twosome from each other. It quickly became a confusion of haphazard battles. Another striking feature of the scene was the close range of each fighting pair, their weapons literally touching or often overlapping despite an effort to separate them.

Robert stood up when he was finished and surveyed his scene. I asked him what he thought of it. "It's a mess!" he declared. I then asked him what he wanted to do about it and he immediately began to reorganize it. He created a wide trench the length of the box. He then separated the soldiers into two sides, "good and bad," and positioned them behind solidly built barriers of sand. When he was finished he stood up, quite pleased, and announced, "Now they're gonna fight." He grabbed a foam encounter bat lying nearby and challenged me to a battle. Encounter bats are two large red foam bats that are soft enough not to hurt when used for battling, but firm enough to satisfy the urge to do so. The rest of his first visit was spent battling me.

After our first visit, Robert's behavior in school changed drastically. His aggression had become focused. When he struck out it was now intentional, and much of the day was spent in a calmer, more reachable state. By reorganizing the chaos of his scene, Robert had reorganized the chaos in him. The profoundness of this cannot be overemphasized. Robert literally restructured himself. His chaotic aggression became focused aggression and it was suddenly possible for him to function. He spent many sessions battling me on many levels, yet his first scene had brought about a real transformation.

Once a sand scene is created, I encourage the child to describe it to me, using the format of a story if they desire. In describing the scene, the child may be describing a central conflict in their lives. The language used is significant. Like the opening scenes of a play in which the basic plot and action to take place are alluded to, so the child's opening scenes offer a glimpse deep into their psyche. At times this glimpse can be hair-raising in the poignant and blunt manner in which it describes the problem. Because the child is protected by the symbol, it can go straight to the heart of the matter, even indicating what needs to happen to rectify the situation. In Robert's case his opening scene presented "the problem" brilliantly by his creating such ineffectual boundaries amidst such chaotically structured aggressive interaction that he himself could witness it as such. His decision to restructure it did just that. By making firm boundaries and two clear sides in the conflict it became possible to utilize all that aggression to some end. Robert arose from his first scene a changed person, ready for further change.

Robert felt both of his parents' histories and the unresolved emotions connected with them. Robert's dealings with peers had an angry desperateness. His dealings with adults usually entailed challenging them when they became too demanding of him. These issues were worked through over time. His parents became involved in their own therapy, which freed Robert from acting out their issues, to a large extent. Eventually Robert's natural aggressiveness became a real asset to him once it was under his control and purged of the pain inflicted by his parents' mistakes.

Seven-year-old Molly came for therapy due to frequent crying in school which was disrupting her classroom and affecting her work. Molly met any amount of frustration, disappointment or stress with tears. Molly had been a very colicky baby and her mother had never been able to console her long enough to forge the type of close bond which she so longed for. Not only was she deeply disappointed in Molly and motherhood in general, but also she took it very personally. After ten months she went back to work to avoid the pain. But this inner tension and grief over her unfulfilled mothering needs very much affected her and her daughter. She had gained a great deal of weight during this frustrating period, which made her feel worse and also angrier.

Molly's father had distanced himself from his wife at this time, becoming overinvolved in his work. He had never really resolved this tendency to avoid by disappearing. Both parents dealt with the stress of being new parents with tendencies they had learned in their own childhoods. As in Robert's case, Molly became entangled in the unresolved aspects of her parents' pasts, as well as the mistakes and circumstances of her own childhood. Molly's tears were not only for herself but for her parents as well. Her parents agreed to work on their problems and went on to do so. But Molly needed to resolve her own problems by taking the important step of being able to express anger without crying. Molly created the following sand scene in her first visit with me:

> A large mountain loomed up in the middle of the box. In one corner there was a deep well ringed by bushes. In the opposite corner a line of women with buckets were leaving a church that was set amidst trees.

Molly described her scene as follows: "A girl lives in the mountain all alone. She is very shy. The women are going to the well to get water."

The scene conveyed two moods, that of isolation and also something mysterious which might occur, that is, loneliness and hope. Whereas Robert reorganized his chaos very quickly, Molly's isolation showed signs of change in her second scene the following week. She again placed a large mountain in the center of the box, with a well in one corner and church in the opposite corner. This time, however, her mountain had a door in it. A path spiraled to the top of the mountain where a knight stood guard. One woman with a bucket now stood by the well. The trees no longer hid the church. We see a basic shift in all three sections of the scene, and we can be sure an inner change is taking place. What had happened inwardly to explain this change? Molly took a very long time to make her scenes and had my undivided attention during this time. Each figure was placed with care. One could see that Molly was experiencing a connection between the objects and her inner self.

In our first visit, after making her scene and with only a few minutes left, Molly eyed the encounter bats I have in my office. She inquired about them tentatively. She was too timid to try them, but did say after giving it much thought that it would be fun to hit her dad with them. Molly had accessed some new energy via her sand scene. Simply stating this desire to aggress allowed Molly to take a step in that direction, judging by her second scene. This sounds very simple and yet it is so.

Molly was stuck at a very infantile level emotionally. She met every frustration with tears, unable to distinguish other ways of expressing herself. Much of what she cried about had actually made her angry, but she had no means of expressing it as such. Explaining this to Molly was helpful as she began to try new forms of self-expression with her family and peers.

Molly stated her case first by proclaiming the isolation she felt as a result of her mother's abandonment. We could say she was stuck in the "mother mountain." The well and the church offered hope, expressing a part of Molly that remained alive and vital. If the well could be reached, perhaps a change could take place. The offer of aggression to which the encounter bats alluded helped energize Molly enough that by her second scene the well had indeed been reached. Here we can see the direct body connection in children's play when it is charged. She came to embody the aggression needed to be angry rather than cry through her first expressing the problem in her opening scene.

After Molly's second scene was made, I suggested we have a paper airplane fight. It was obvious that she was eager to aggress, which means after all "to move towards or forward" but simply afraid of the intensity of this desire. She accepted the airplane fight readily. This allowed her to use some of the muscles and impulses involved in more direct combat, but with the safety of distance and lightness. By using the same muscles but with a slightly different emphasis, she was able to experience her aggression in a tolerable dose. This made the next step easier. She left very happy.

In her third scene Molly again began with a central mountain. This time though there was a window and a doormat in front of the door. The guard was gone and a car was parked nearby. At one point a girl appeared in the window, the girl, looking out. To describe how amazing it was to have the girl herself appear at the window is impossible. For a fleeting moment it seemed to be her very soul peering out from the mountain. Molly felt awed by it momentarily and then moved on, as children must do.

y didn't elaborate on the scene but rather utilized the girl's
:e and the new energy it brought to the surface in her. She stood up
.... .... :ager to try the encounter bats. When her father arrived to pick her
up, she was hiding behind the door with an encounter bat and jumped out at
him with glee. From this point on Molly's scenes were very different. The
mountain was gone. The girl had emerged.

Of all materials sand is the most like the psyche, and also much like the
body, especially the child's body that is still forming and malleable. The
physical-psychic link here is very strong. The sand's depth, malleability and
porosity allow for many levels of self-expression. Things can be hidden in it,
deep or right below the surface. Objects can sink into it or emerge out of it.
Early childhood experiences, especially traumatic ones and their accompanying feelings, often sink into the unconscious, still influencing us greatly
though beyond our conscious grasps. The sand duplicates the unconscious,
providing a format for awakening. The sand can be made firm with the
addition of water or it can remain loose. The four walls of the box provide a
boundary for this complex substance. Combine this with an adult witness
who is unafraid and nonjudgmental of the material buried in the child's
unconscious and who appreciates its symbolic expression and importance,
and the results can be astounding.

Sandplay is an intensely physical experience for children. Many children
begin to show signs of this as soon as they put their hands into the sand.
Their breathing deepens or changes in some perceptible way. They may even
pant as they set to work. They become flushed as if exerting great physical
effort. They often pass gas or have to run to the bathroom soon after
beginning to use it. This is especially true in their early sand scenes when
things are still more blocked in them. I think this physical response is a result
of things loosening up. It is a very good sign. It may be that a therapist who is
open to the child's physicality will either notice it more and/or encourage it
simply by their unspoken attitude.

Mark, aged six, was brought for therapy due to school phobia. Although
never enthusiastic about going to school, or secure once there, his resistance
had escalated. He had no friends and was unwilling to go through the social
steps necessary to make them, such as having children over to his house or
vice versa.

When Mark was a toddler his father had been extremely violent towards
his mother in Mark's presence. Although his mother had since divorced him,
Mark's father still saw him on a monthly basis and Mark's mother was still

frightened of him. Mark had a permanent look of shock on his face, which under stress easily turned to a look of terror.

In my experience, perhaps the most damaging experience a young boy can endure is to have his mother abused by his father. He will either wind up identifying with his father out of fear and grow up hating woman (and himself unconsciously), or as in the case of Mark he will turn his natural aggression on himself and his own developing ego. Either way it is a difficult situation to remedy.

Fathers represent the world to children, the world of doing and relating, even today when most mothers work. It is easy to see how Mark's early trauma around his father might make him reject the world and feel anxious about separation from his mother and his home. That Mark's father was quite famous and admired by many made it harder still. Mark was quite candid in our first meeting about his school difficulties. The children in school were not always nice. He was unable to react towards them with any amount of aggression, even verbally. The potentially negative effects of male aggression had been made clear to him as a young child and he had become afraid of his own aggression as a result. Yet to grow we must be able to aggress or else become immobilized. His only recourse was to withdraw. He was too frozen with fear and inhibition when I first met him to do otherwise.

His first sand scene consisted of four separate mountains. On top of the first mountain was a forest with a bear in it. On top of the second mountain was a village. On the third was a castle with a group of knights guarding it. The fourth mountain was bare. This bare mountain was the focus of Mark's energy and the scene's "charge." When he described the scene he revealed that inside of the bare mountain lived horrible monsters.

Mark's first monster, which I asked him to make at our session's onset, was very tiny. Its head was so small there was no room for features. He was extremely uncomfortable making it, partly because he felt he wasn't good at drawing and didn't like to do things he wasn't naturally good at, and partly because of what doing so represented to him. His drawing was hardly visible just as the monsters in the scene were invisible. Yet even the indication that they existed, which came from Mark, allowed for the beginning of change.

Mark's second scene duplicated the first except that the bare mountain had several shells on it. These were actually covering up monsters that Mark had stuck beneath them. After Mark described the scene to me, he slowly and dramatically lifted up each shell and let the monsters out. This lifting of the shells was a very dramatic moment. Mark was lifting the lid off of his own blocked aggression in that moment. A door was now open within him.

This action activated the entire scene. First the knights came down from their mountain to fight the monsters. The village came to life and the groups of animals began to run around. A group of buffaloes, which Mark nicknamed the "head-butters," began banging heads and thus became the scene's focus.

Mark named each of the buffaloes after the key males in his life (minus his father), including himself. Only the bear in the forest remained unchanged.

When Mark let the monsters out, the energy released by this was palpable. Mark became very animated. After finishing his scene, Mark battled me with the encounter bats. He even experimented with being a "head-butter," charging at me from across the room and crashing into a pillow that I held. This was orchestrated by me but sparked by Mark.

In Mark's life after his second scene, his school phobia stopped. He went to school willingly, if not enthusiastically. It took Mark many more sessions to embody the energy which his scenes had activated. He consciously resisted the idea of aggression, even as it began to manifest in his life. Self-assertion with his peers was slower in coming, yet his teacher saw him as less guarded and more alive.

One symbol that Mark used is worth looking at: that is the symbol of the bear. Present and unchanging in Mark's early scenes, always placed in the scene first, it was obviously important to Mark. I think of the bear as a symbol of instinctual wisdom. I have read of the prevalence of bear cults in various parts of the ancient world, and in these cults the bear was worshipped and bear meat eaten ritualistically by all members of the village, communion-like.

This harkens back to the story "The Giant Bear" told in Chapter 1 (p.21). Looked at in light of this, Mark's bear symbol makes great sense. By using a symbol that collectively has represented power, he was accessing this collective power and joining with others in doing so; stepping out of the isolated place he had become locked in.

Mark imbued his scenes with an importance that affected him on a very deep level. He went on over time to separate from his mother, bond with peers, and become aggressive when needed. The bear, with its grounded power, reflects the inner wisdom and strength to do so.

Mark's opening scenes made use of one of the sand's most interesting qualities. He alluded to something existing beneath the sand and was later able to place it there and bring it forth like planting a seed and seeing it take root and grow. In these moments we are actually witnessing an absent or repressed aspect of the self take form and come into consciousness. When a girl comes to the window or monsters emerge from their shells, we know a deep change is occurring. We will hear it reflected in the feedback we receive from parents or school. We will see it reflected in the child's face, posture and manner of relating to the world.

One child I worked with, William, always made two worlds in the sand. The visible world on the sand's surface was neat and organized but lifeless. The other world he only alluded to. "It's beneath the sand and goes on for miles and is so beautiful," he would tell me in a whispered voice. Slowly this deeper world began to be visible in his scenes and likewise the more vital part of himself became more apparent in his person. In one session an earth-quake blasted both worlds to bits, intermingling them as a result. He was now integrated, no longer divided.

Another child referred in her description of her opening sand scene to other places that her characters came from and went to, expanding the story as she did this and also herself. The box couldn't contain the whole world of the story as it was too big and complex, but she creatively adapted to this. The real action and danger of the story took place "there" and the character and story were also transformed "there." When the main female character in the story came back from "there" she and her life were changed, as was the little girl who made the scene.

All of the children mentioned thus far accessed energy via their play, whether it was in the charged scenes created in their sandplay or the expressive play that emerged from these scenes. No other medium offers the variety and complexity of metaphors for growth and transformation as the sand. It facilitates the emergence of a new life-affirming energy that the child will use to become whole.

Chapter 4

# Energy

Whether drawing monsters, creating sand scenes, pounding at clay, enacting spontaneous fantasies, or attacking me with encounter bats, the key to change in working therapeutically with children is accessing energy. Symbols are "energy laden," as we have already seen. Their relevance to us is their energy. The difference between a beautiful picture and a symbolic one is in the latter's containment of energy, which when accessed will bring about change (Figure 4.1).

*Figure 4.1 An energy-laden picture*

The word "energy" is synonymous with vitality and aliveness. If we think of energy as the manifestation of one's aliveness, then the movement of it throughout the organism, the amount and availability of it to the individual, becomes important.

## Pulsation

Wilhelm Reich was the first western doctor and psychiatrist to speak of energy and its relationship to health. It has formed the basis of oriental medicine for centuries. Reich spoke of energy not as a psychic precept but as an actual, measurable force, which provides the organism with the ability to function. He believed that a disturbance in the energetic flow was at the basis of all individual and social ills: "This energy governs the entire organism; it is expressed in the emotions as well as in the purely biophysical movements of the organs" (Reich 1945, p.356). Reich saw this energy as "pulsatory," an expansion and contraction, as evident in respiration, peristalsis, and the beating of the heart. A simple experiment with an amoeba demonstrates this pulsation, observable through a microscope. Energy builds up in the amoeba, creating a charged state. The energy is discharged and the amoeba relaxes. The cycle begins again. The amoeba is never still. Normal expansion is exaggerated when the amoeba reaches out for food. The reverse action, or a contraction, occurs when the amoeba is attacked by the environment. If attacked repeatedly, the amoeba expands more cautiously and anxiously. If the attacks continue the amoeba stays contracted, in a state of defense. If the attacks persist beyond this, the amoeba will lose energy, shrivel up and die (Baker 1967). We can begin to see the basis of emotional health and emotional disorders via this experiment.

The movements of the amoeba in its free-flow state actually look much like the natural movements of an infant. We can observe the infant reaching out with eyes, mouth and eventually hands for contact and food. We can observe the infant contract in response to a sharp sound or an unpleasant sensation, such as a wet diaper. However simple the amoeba's functioning may seem in comparison to that of humans, we can begin to understand energy and the energetic process in all living things by observing it. The ability to expand and contract, or to pulsate, is synonymous with life. In Reich's words: "If the biological oscillation is disturbed in one direction or the other, i.e. the function of expansion or the function of contraction pre-dominates, then there must be a disturbance of the general biological balance" (Reich 1973, p.266).

Because expansion is synonymous with pleasure and contraction with anxiety, we can begin to see the effects of a negative growth environment on a child at the most basic level of existence. It is inevitable that life will cause us to contract, and it is actually a necessary part of the cycle. When contraction dominates and upsets the balance, we have the capacity to emote, which reinstates the natural flow of aliveness. Literally defined, the word emotion means "moving outward or pushing out." We must take the word literally, then, in order to understand how our emotions work to maintain health.

Dr. Alexander Lowen, a student of Reich's and pioneer in his own right, developed a system of working energetically with patients called Bio-energetics Analysis. Bioenergy again refers to the energy of life, which provides us with the ability to function. At the basis of all human structures, which Lowen envisions as a pyramid, on the deepest body level are the energetic processes that activate the person. These energetic processes express themselves through movements, which give rise to feelings, which result in thoughts. Ego, the crown of the pyramid, arises out of all that is below it (Lowen 1990). To have a healthy ego, the lower, deeper layers of the pyramid must be accessible. All that is below the level of conscious thought, which in Lowen's model is most of the person, continues to affect us even if we ignore it, and especially if we do so. The therapist who sees only the top layers of the person doesn't really see the person.

Pulsation is respiration, peristalsis, the beating of the heart and other bodily functions. Behaviorally, pulsation manifests itself in reaching out and pulling back. Reaching out leads to contact with the self. To be static in either is pathological since life depends on pulsation, the ability to move out or withdraw as the situation requires (Lowen 1990).

Pulsation in human beings is most evident in the experience of the orgasm. Both Reich and Lowen saw the "orgasm reflex" as crucial to emotional health. The orgasm reflex is a four-point process – tension, charge, discharge, relaxation – which more than any other form of discharge helps to maintain health.

This charge–discharge formula relates to all of life's energetic experi-ences. It is present in storms and volcanic eruptions and also in the smallest microscopic organisms such as the amoeba. It describes the simplest and largest of life's processes and it pertains to the child also, insomuch as the mechanism that realizes itself via orgasm in the adolescent and adult operates in the child, but in the form and service of growth. This process begins at conception, at the onset of life. It will come to include a sexual awakening in adolescence but is present as simple pulsation throughout our childhood, especially in our play. Most of the play sessions I have witnessed follow this model when they are alive, when the child is engaged with them-selves and their play, when the play feels like a change is occurring via it.

Reich and Lowen examined in depth the human capacity for pleasure and expansion culminating in orgasm and the healthy sexual embrace, as well as the many cultural, familial and individual means of interfering with this. In both Reich's and Lowen's approach the energetic contractions and "blocks" which form the basis of unhappiness are dealt with through a combination of verbal analysis and physical pressure. The latter can take the form of deep muscular pressure or physical exercises and positions which not only help manifest where the blocks are, but also may help release the repressed emotions therein. Released too, often in the form of memories, is information regarding the origins of these blocks, which brings a deeper level of self-awareness. Pressure is also put on a person's defenses by confronting them as they manifest in the therapeutic interaction. For example, the person may have a tendency to smile or look blank when speaking about something very upsetting. By confronting this defense and manipulating the musculature involved in maintaining it, the person will have access to feelings and energy previously unavailable. The smile may mask tears or rage, both of which when acknowledged and expressed will begin to reinstate some aspect of the self.

In working with children the technique is very different, although the underlying process and end result are the same. I don't usually engage children in a verbal interchange regarding their situation, although sometimes at a key point it can be very helpful. I don't confront children directly but rather encourage them to try things that I know will be provocative and require a change in their defenses, such as monster drawing. Pressure is primarily exerted on the child's defenses by the very play configurations that they themselves often chose to undertake. As a result they can release and access the energy needed to change with a rapidity that is at times startling. Eventually in a child's play, if it is "charged" with the life energy needed to bring about change, we will begin to see pulsation.

The idea of "charged" play is the core of dynamic play therapy. When a scene or any play configuration is charged it means that some energy has surfaced in the context of the play and in the child's body-psyche. This is palpable to the therapist who is open to it. Many things may happen as a result. Cathartic play may ensue. The story or play may become suddenly more alive, more purposeful, and the child will also as a result. The play may begin to pulsate.

As we work energetically with children in the play therapy process we witness this pulsating growth process again and again. It is the central tenet of my approach, the looked for sign that real transformation is happening. It is often subtle, occurring over the course of several sessions, or happening in the sandbox, or a particular drawing or symbol the child is using. It is always present where change is.

Five-year-old Josh began therapy after years of medical trauma. A serious chronic illness had sent him to emergency rooms on many occasions, where he was subjected to numerous blood tests each time. These were often administered with great insensitivity. Josh's parents were very loving and devoted to him. Seeing their son ravaged by illness and insensitive caregivers had left them devastated. They lived in constant fear of his becoming ill and this, combined with frequent periods of illness, had frozen Josh energetically. Periodic fits of rage would temporarily release this frozen state. He had been unwilling to toilet train and was becoming unwilling to defecate at all, which precipitated his parents bringing him for therapy.

Josh entered the play setting wide-eyed with terror, yet eager on some level to play. He had been told that I had a sandbox in my office. The act of playing, which is itself a symbol of aliveness for the child, has the power to overshadow the child's fears. This thrust towards health is evident in most children.

Josh's body had a small, frail, anemic look to it – in some way fetus-like. His head was disproportionately large for the rest of his body. He shook my hand when his mother first introduced us, and the quality of his hand energetically was cold and lifeless.

Josh approached the sandbox after a moment and immediately began to play in it. At my request he made a scene, which was as follows. Several people, houses and trees were set into the sand, creating a pastoral look. Then Josh informed me that beneath the sand a fire was raging and it was about to erupt. He was checking to see if it was all right with me for the eruption to occur. The scene and his relationship, as well as the space around the sandbox we both inhabited, were suddenly "charged." I knew something was coming. He then began to blast large amounts of sand into the air covering all the objects he had placed there. He repeated these eruptions again and again, and began to pass large amounts of gas with his body as he did so. He continued this for the entire visit.

When he left at the end of the session he looked relaxed and happy. That week he began using the toilet at home and in a few weeks it was a normal part of his life. In Josh's case his emotional condition had a physical basis. Metabolism provides the energy that results in movement. Obviously when metabolism is reduced, as in illness, motility is decreased. This relationship works in reverse also. Any decrease in the body's motility affects its metabolism:

The intimate connection between breathing, moving and feeling is known to the child but is generally ignored by the adult. Children learn that holding the breath cuts off unpleasant sensations and feelings. They suck in their bellies and immobilize their diaphragms to reduce anxiety. They lie very still to avoid feeling afraid. They deaden their bodies in order not to feel pain. (Lowen 1970, p.39)

We can see a very clear example of this in Josh's case. Josh's parents' childhoods had been very traumatic. Each of them had been sexually molested and each had kept it a secret their whole lives. In working with them on relaxing and letting go so that Josh could grow, this information came to light. It explained the severity of their reaction to their son's trauma. Although their overprotectiveness of Josh had in many ways been advantageous, their mood of fear and helplessness was actually thwarting their son's growth and his state of health.

His parents relaxing a bit and the positive use Josh made of his play therapy sessions brought about a striking increase in his ability to fight off illness. He succeeded in avoiding emergency rooms for the duration of his therapy and beyond.

Initially Josh's sessions all took place at the sandbox. It was as if the rest of the room didn't exist. After his initial "erupting" scene, all of Josh's sandplay involved bulls as the main characters. The bull became his totem, so to speak. I have numerous bulls in my miniature collection and Josh used them all, usually as a group of comrades fighting a variety of foes that were always invisible.

These battles grew in intensity and loudness as Josh grew. I was both his witness and his assistant, an integral part of the process and yet peripheral to it as well. Josh grew by leaps and bounds during this period, which further encouraged his parents to relax and let go.

Eventually the action of his scenes began to spill out into the rest of the room, literally. The battles became so intense that they required more space, using the floor and various pieces of furniture throughout the room. This paralleled and precipitated a period of physical and social expansion in Josh's life. He began to try new things at home, such as sleeping in his own bed alone and making new friends.

Throughout this period the bull was the constant heroic symbol. In the last session I had with Josh, he created a scene that was again limited to the sandbox and strikingly different in scope. A new *human* hero appeared.

Before going into battle he would ritualistically eat one of his pet bulls, thereby having "the power of the bull inside of him" as Josh informed me.

This brought to mind the use of the sacrificial bull in ancient and even in contemporary religious rites. This primitive communion ritual certainly made sense with Josh. His body now reflected the strength and aliveness of his favorite symbol.

The situations that cause children to deaden themselves are numerous. The holding environment that parents provide can be too weak or too restrictive. It can be too stimulating, thereby overcharging the child, or too understimulating, thereby leaving the child unsatisfied and ungrounded. Using Reich's and Lowen's ideas we can begin to look at children energetically, trying to understand how they have been affected, and, more important, how they can release, unthaw, etc. Is there too little or too much energy in the child? How alive do they seem? How afraid of their aliveness are they? How chaotic or how still is this energy? If we look at and listen to and perceive the child with our own sensory apparatus along these lines we can assess what is going on and what direction we need to go in.

If we recall James from Chapter 2, whose "slipping and falling" play brought about such a change in his level of functioning and the almost immediate disappearance of his wetting and soiling himself, we can look at the changes it brought about in his body as well. James's musculature at the onset of therapy was undefined, the way an infant looks prior to mastering mobility and uprightness. This was manifest not only in the shape of his musculature but also in the first impulse to play that he expressed through falling and standing. Although James had mastered physical mobility to some degree he had obviously not mastered the psychological aspects that being upright awaken. I suspect that James's mother hovered too close while he learned to stand, making it her victory rather than his. By losing his footing when he slipped on the ice and dragging me down with him, he playfully enacted a wonderful reversal of what had happened to him, giving him a chance to rectify it. When he stood on his two feet after so much theatrical slipping he was really standing on *his* two feet.

By the termination of James's therapy, approximately two months in length, his body had changed drastically. His musculature had elongated and become defined, calling to mind the snake he drew at the end of each visit, which grew longer and longer until it began to contract and grow teeth. Here we see pulsation in action, expanding slowly as his snake grew from his slipping capers, and then contracting slowly into a fierce and highly energized creature. Energetically, by mobilizing his aggression, pulsation was able to express itself fully in the service of growth. He could then reach out to his peers and not remain immersed in the mother matrix. The fear and inhibition that were impeding growth had been discharged. He went on to be a leader among his peers, a highly successful athlete and a very self-possessed young man.

Contraction and expansion (or pulsation) are apparent in the entire process of therapy with children, in my experience. Children's very use of the play modality follows this pattern. Sandplay and the use of the sandbox is paradoxical in that it seems to have a quality of contraction and concentratedness, and yet also, due to its amorphous and very flexible nature, it can just as easily manifest and express expansion.

When I first began to observe pulsation in children's play I assumed it was coincidental. But after many years of seeing it in subtle and often not so subtle ways I have recognized it for what it is: the life force at work that serves the function of changing the child energetically, or bringing the change to the surface. During play sessions when this apparent expansion and contraction is obviously occurring it extends beyond the individual session hour. I have children end one session with their play configuration expanded out into the space, filling up the room to the maximum, only to return several weeks later and resume their play from this edge of the room in an expanded state. The scenes that take place in the midst of this pulsatory play will "feel" different, much more dynamic and alive as if the box and the room have become part of a living organism.

I have even observed this pulsatory process in supervising other therapists who have no awareness of such a phenomenon nor interest in it. One therapist showed me a series of slides of the sand scenes of one very abused child she had worked with. When looked at sequentially the content of each scene slowly grew and moved toward the periphery of the box and then withdrew into the center, often into a very tight center. Then snakes would appear and the scenes would slowly expand again.

Sometimes this phenomenon happens in other aspects of a child's play. It may show up in the block configurations they make, the clay figures or drawings they create, or in their use of the space itself. One child alternated in his sessions between very concentrated play in one sandbox to sessions in which he used all of the several rooms I have in my office suite. He called this expansive play "interplanetary travel." Then he would once again pull into a tight, more focused phase of play in one box. Again, aside from the obvious expanding and contracting that was visible, this phase of his play coincided with great changes in his life.

After a period of contracted play, the release which follows may expand out of the sandbox or it may take place within the safety net of the sand container, as in Josh's fire which erupted from beneath the surface of the sand but not out into the room in the form of movement or more aggressive play. For many children the entire process takes place in the box, the expansion and contraction occurring in all their ramifications within the four walls of it. The energetic experience, however, is the same. Once we are attuned to this pulsation, we see it more and more, in many of children's play experiences that might otherwise not seem like much. It may even be referred to rather than shown in the sand.

One girl recently informed me, after making a very pretty and peaceful scene with a female character setting out on a journey at its centerpiece, that in another part of the land there was danger that the boundaries might be threatened. The main female character was going there to stand guard. After a while she told me that other members of the tribe were going to help her. So the scene expanded into an area that was invisible, yet it felt like and was a true expansion of this child's physical and psychic experience of herself. I believe there was a significant cognitive shift in that moment.

Four-year-old Chris had begun throwing tantrums at home on a regular basis. These tantrums might occur several times a day and last up to one hour in length. He had also become resistant to leaving home in general – especially for the preschool he attended twice per week, or babysitters. Once he was actually at these places he was fine, but the prelude was exhausting to him and his mother, and also dangerous as the tantrums often happened in the car. In other ways Chris was oppositional too. He had resisted any efforts at toilet training and yet usually had tantrums about having his diapers changed.

These behaviors had emerged or intensified after a very difficult year between Chris's parents. They had spent the year embroiled in marital difficulties with frequent loud fights and threats of divorce. The children were often the subject of their fights, if not the real reason for them. Chris's older brother became the focus of his father's rage and the effect of this on Chris was to make him ambivalent about growing older himself. During the worst period of his parents' fighting, Chris was if anything overly passive. Within weeks of his parents' difficulties having begun to be resolved via therapy, Chris began to have tantrums.

Chris entered the play space with ease, to his mother's surprise. He let her leave and began playing in the sandbox, organizing a fight between "a good guy" and many bad guys. Chris was a solid, compact little boy. As he played, his face, body, and voice were expressive of all that he was experiencing. His face would contract with anger when the good guy was attacked. The attacker would then be tossed into the air and Chris would throw his head back and explode into laughter. Sometimes the contraction would be in his jaw, sometimes his eyes and at other times his fists. The release of tossing away the enemy came with increasing gusto.

Suddenly Chris jumped up and grabbed my hand very tightly. "There's a monster in there!" he whispered, pointing to a closet door in my office. "What should we do?" I asked him. "Let's go scare him!" was his reply. So we crept to the closet door, flung it open and, following Chris's lead, roared at the top of our lungs. This was repeated many times in each of the several doorways in my office. Then we returned to the sand for a period of concentrated fighting.

The fear in Chris as he grabbed my hand was very real, as was the release he felt by flinging open the door and roaring. This episode was repeated several times. The contrast between the sandplay, which felt like a squeezed fist, and the confrontation with the monsters, which was an enormous expansion, was striking. Chris's body was "charged" as we approached the door. This allowed for the intensification of the release and also its relevance to him on both an energetic and emotional level.

During this type of play the office becomes an extension of the child's own body, psyche and energetic field. It is a very important and quite exhilarating experience. The child will leave much more relaxed and happier, if not fully resolved. A huge piece of fear will have been removed along with the need for the oppositional behavior that the child uses to defend herself in the face of fear.

In the following weeks Chris's mother let him spend more time at home, honoring his genuine need to recoup some nurturing time with her that had long been missing. At the same time his father, whom he was very close to, engaged him in a positive and successful toilet training campaign. Meanwhile he came to play a few more times, repeating with variations his playful yet emotionally genuine discharge of fear and rage.

In all the sand scenes described in Chapter 3, there was an expression of aggression afterwards. This is often true when the symbolic expression has been therapeutic, when the energy has been accessed. The child then needs to do something with this new energy. A child may challenge me to a fight of some sort, or wish to bounce upon the mattress, or build a tower of blocks and smash it down. Or the scene itself may erupt into an aggressive outpouring as in Josh's case. This is an essential part of the process. If we call to mind that aggression means "movement towards" we can see it as the equivalent of reaching out of the self towards the world.

## Grounding

The energy that Lowen and Reich speak of and that I have been observing and helping children to access all these years needs to be grounded. One of Lowen's most important contributions to our knowledge and treatment of individuals is the concept of *grounding*. Lowen likened the body to an electronic devise that needs to be connected to the ground so that any surge of energy affecting the system funnels the excess energy into the ground rather than into the device itself. For humans, surges come in the form of fluctuations in the flow of excitation and in the emotions. Not only the so-called negative emotions of anger, fear and sadness, but even the positive emotion of pleasure are experienced as a surge on an organismic level, and in the ungrounded individual are threatening to their sense of integrity. The physical symptoms of children with neurological disorders, for example, are often as exacerbated by a positive sensation or situation as they are by a negatively stressful one. Although fear is certainly experienced as very different than pleasure, they both excite the organism.

Humans ground primarily through their legs and feet, which serve the function of roots in a sense (Lowen 1990). Babies and young children will often ground against their parents' bodies, pushing their feet into their bellies while nursing, or pushing against their legs while beginning to stand. In a sense they use us, if they are able to, as their ground wires until they are able to stand on their own two feet. They rely on us as a result to help them discharge, to reinstate equilibrium. I believe these simple acts of grounding through a parent's body are some of our first experiences of intimacy. In these moments of pushing against another the child experiences not only its own body more solidly but the other's body as well. The same thing happens in adolescence when children again need to push against us to know themselves better. Then too we as parents need to be a solid and yet flexible grounding medium.

James the "ice-slipper" found the ground by losing a false sense of ground. As he did so he could better handle his own energy, his own aggression and that of his peers. James found his legs and his ability to stand on his own by exaggerating the symptom. By losing his footing completely on the ice, as a very young child might often do, James addressing the problem of "I can't stand up on my own two feet" in a manner that not only expressed this well and even playfully, but allowed him while down on the ground to find a way of getting up. It was both problem and solution in one. He could then go forth into life with a solid sense of himself.

As children become upright and feel their own solidity, they enter that marvelous but maddening to most parents phase known as "the terrible twos" in which they begin to discharge on their own, feeling the power and beginnings of individuality that come from their own relationship with the ground. When the child begins to feel this power they begin to use us to push against in a different way. At this stage it becomes more about self-awareness, more about them and less about a shared experience.

I have a mattress in my office for pounding and jumping on and a mini-trampoline as well. These offer a means of solidifying the sense of ground. The sand is also a wonderful grounding tool as it is on the ground and of the ground. When children manipulate it, they are experiencing the same feelings that they have when they jump to some extent. More so the sand relates to a sense of inner or psychic ground, and the layers of soil that contain all of our human capabilities. This ground stirs up ancient genetic memories, what Carl Jung called "the two million year old man" in us. And the child affirms their humanity and grounds in it as they play.

## Cathartic play

I have a tennis racket for hitting the mattress with, and encounter bats for hitting me with. They offer a direct means of expressing the aggression as well as the anger which therapeutic play brings to the surface. Most children find this very satisfying and rarely exhibit any inhibition towards doing so. Some children are not ready at the onset of therapy to use these tools. Like Molly and Mark from the previous chapter, these children need to access their aggression through their imaginations first. The act of aggressing may have too many negative connotations, or else it means separating from a parent the child is still holding on to, still unresolved about.

They need to find the basis of this aggression themselves and the sandbox with its protective four walls and the amorphous form of the sand itself allow this to happen in an initially more indirect way. Once a child is engaged in a direct discharge, I will often ask them where they feel the anger in their bodies and encourage them to use this part of their anatomy in expressing it. Thus some children prefer jumping on to the mattress, feeling great power in using their feet. Others enjoy flinging themselves at it, using their whole body.

Cathartic play always looks aggressive, in that it expresses pent-up emotions and energy in what is a "moving forward or towards" sense. This aggressive cathartic moment will feel very intense to the witnessing therapist as well. Even in very young children, latent or thwarted energy is exhilarating to watch as it explodes forth in play.

A six-year-old girl came to see me in the wake of her parents informing her that they would be getting divorced. They had never fought in front of her so it was a total surprise. She had always been a rather pleasantly passive child, and this would not do considering the state of upheaval her life was now in and the feelings she must be having inside. She began to create a repetitive scene in the sand in which a monster attacked a compound guarded by soldiers. At first the monster just made forays to examine the fort, taunting the soldiers and people therein. But after a few sessions of this taunting play the monster began to eat all the people. It would then vomit up all of them and eat them again. As this small child described vocally this repetitive devouring and vomiting I began to feel nauseous. As I sat with my own visceral reaction and witnessed her monster's antics I realized that underneath the nausea was fear and rage, and that it was what she was feeling. The minute I got this the intensity of her play increased in volume and became really cathartic rather than repetitive. My own feeling of nausea immediately ceased. She was not always so pleasant at home after this, but I am told she weathered the subsequent months well as a result.

With her, the bodily and emotional basis to her play was very clear. There was little division between the drama in the box and the drama inside her. The body's natural tendency is often to vomit when experiencing a strong affect, especially in a state of shock, as she must have been. When I recognized what she must be feeling it was communicated immediately to her without me saying a word. We can't make a child engage on the very deep level this child did. We can, however, know that it is possible and needed, that is, have a vision of how things might be, offer materials and a safe space where it can happen, and if possible use our own bodily reactions to better understand the child.

If a therapist doesn't allow for cathartic play, which a great many do not, they will not be able to truly help a child in any deep sense of the word. Many therapists who work with children are reluctant to let them truly express themselves in an energetic sense. They play board games or a subdued and intellectualized form of play therapy. They express a fear of unleashing aggression in the children they are treating, but I believe they are really afraid of their own monsters growling beneath the surface of their body and psyche. It is probably wise to avoid this type of play therapy if one has not encountered one's own monster or at least begun the process of doing so, simply because our fear of it will make us ineffectual in joining with and assisting the child's energy. Then they will be alone with their monster, like the child whose night-time fears are treated as nonsense. But if we are to help bring about deep change and facilitate the individuation process we must be willing to open the door and encounter the monsters in ourselves. Then dragons may be slain and resurrected and so will the child's wounded spirit that is still alive even if it is now hidden in symptoms.

In our work with children we should be concerned not with simply turning out "good" children (i.e., obedient ones), but rather with attempting to reinstate the natural sense of grace and flow inherent in all living creatures, and to re-establish the child's natural capacity to love, both oneself and others. Real goodness can only exist if someone has at least an inkling of the ferocious forces that dwell in our psyches and is able to modulate their expression, not through repression but understanding. For the very power that goodness implies needs these deeper forces aligned with it. I find that when children express their aggression and even their violent impulses via therapy they are soon able to be more genuinely loving in their lives. Many a child has come and made a sibling out of clay and chopped them up repeatedly only to go home and be able to relate better to the very same sibling.

When these wilder more unacceptable emotions have a place in which they are accepted and can be expressed in a contained, grounded way, they do not run amok but rather the energy of the negative infuses the positive. This is the key to my work with children, accentuating the negative so that it becomes a part of the child and not anti them.

Chapter 5

# The Power of No

Many years ago, on a trip with my family to visit the ruins of ancient Delphi in Greece, the site of the famous oracle, our tour guide and self-appointed oracle told the following story. During World War II the Italian dictator Mussolini wrote a letter to the Greek president encouraging him to join the fascists' side in the war. His long, eloquent and demanding letter was answered with a one-word note: "Ochi," which means "No." In Greece this letter is commemorated each year on Ochi day or the day of No. It is a day of celebration of an act of defiance in the face of corrupt authority.

It is possible to categorize most of the children I have worked with under two headings: those who are unable to say no, and those who are unable not to say no. In both cases, no is the issue. When children are unable to say no, the no is still present but buried beneath the surface of the psyche and the body. The ways this unspoken no may manifest itself are numerous. Most of the children described in the preceding chapters fall under this heading. Some of them expressed the no with their bowels and bladders, others through withdrawal and/or passivity. Still others expressed it through school or social difficulties. Meanwhile, their parents often described them as "good" children in every other respect.

Children who come in with symptoms such as enuresis, encopresis or self-stimulation have usually had problems all along, but with the emergence of these offensive symptoms the cry for help is heard. In other words, when the no begins to manifest itself in a way that is more offensive, it alerts the world around the child that something is wrong. This is, after all, one of the functions of no, and also one of the functions of symptoms. The no functions like a psychological membrane that parallels a physiological membrane, such as the skin, in its purpose. No prevents the individual from being overwhelmed by outside pressures. It allows for discrimination. It allows for impulse control. It defines the ego boundaries of an individual. It helps filter out what is good from what is bad for the organism. It affirms what are "I" and "not I" (Lowen 1970).

The infant expresses no with its reflexes. The startle reflex is one example in which the entire organism says no. The gag reflex is another example, the body's means of preventing unwanted and unhealthy matter from entering. Negative emotions such as crying and anger when expressed are forms of no, reinstating pleasure through the release of tension or by alerting our parents or caretakers that something is wrong, which when corrected will lead to pleasure.

Many children's defense systems become organized around the word no in a more apparent way. They say it loudly via their oppositional or provocative behavior. They express it by being disruptive, stubborn, resistant or violent. In a way, these children seem healthier at first glance. They often seem to display a higher level of aliveness. If one has grown up afraid to say no, these children seem more functional. Yet they too are stuck and in pain. In the long run it is not any easier for them to resolve their difficulties. To be stuck in *no* is to strip it of its discriminatory function. For these children the process of therapy involves a surrendering, a giving up of the battle once it is possible to do so and maintain a sense of integrity. Interestingly, these children often create monsters in their opening sessions that are not violent or grotesque but rather helpful. For them it is the noble, heroic part of the self that is repressed and turned into something conflictual.

It is ironic that developmentally the age of no, approximately two years of age, is commonly called "the terrible twos." Later on we urge our children to say no: "Say no to drugs" or "Say no to strangers." But when it is developmentally essential that the child express the no we label the whole period as terrible. Certainly the need for containment and guidance on the part of the parent is as important with a boisterous, no-saying two-year-old as with any other childhood stage. Yet if the ability to say no is thwarted by punishment, rejection or guilt, or by a lack of containment, our sense of self is greatly diminished. It is helpful to hear once again Lowen's statement quoted in Chapter 1:

> Knowledge is a function of discrimination. To know what A is, it must be distinguished from all that is not A. Knowledge arises from the recognition of differences. The first difference that an organism can recognize is that between what feels good to the body or pleasurable and what feels painful. (Lowen 1970, p.155)

The child begins to express and assert this discrimination when able to artic-ulate the no. In Eric Erikson's book *Childhood and Society*, he lists the ego qualities that emerge from critical periods of development and which are essential to healthy functioning. The age of no, roughly two years of age, he describes as the age of Autonomy vs. Shame and Doubt. If autonomy, that is, being self-governing, is not mastered and integrated in the developing ego, the result is a pervasive sense of shame and doubt. Further, "if denied the gradual and well-guided experience of the autonomy of free choice…the child will turn against himself all his urge to discriminate and to manipulate" (Erikson 1950, p.252). If we look back over the children presented thus far we can see this manifest in the symptoms and demeanor of each child. The monsters they drew in their opening sessions indicated some of what each child was internalizing or turning within.

If we look at the drawings shown in this book in terms of this internal-ization process, they take on a new and deeper meaning. The urgent need for the feelings and energy that they represent to be expressed becomes more obvious. They will wreak havoc of some sort in the child's life, for they are a force that will not go away (Figure 5.1).

*Figure 5.1 A nine-year-old boy imagines his monster devouring his father*

A healthy no is a precursor to a healthy yes. To give of the self one must feel the self, knowing one's boundaries and limits, which the no asserts and helps to clarify. Over the entrance to the temple of Apollo at Delphi, those seeking the god's advice and wisdom were greeted with two admonishments: "Know thyself" and "Nothing in excess." The interrelationship between these two pearls of wisdom is their basis in the capacity to say no. To know is based in being able to say *no*.

The following case is an example of a child whose "no" was external, worn like a suit of armor which by the time I began working with him was truly jeopardizing his health. Michael, age six, was referred by the summer day camp he was attending. He was spending most of each day there crying, demanded constant one-on-one attention and refused to participate in any activities.

In a meeting with Michael's parents it turned out he was still in diapers. He had developed a terror of the toilet at age two and a half and had refused to use it. This coincided with the birth of a sibling. He had been in therapy in the nearby city where he lived during the school year, but to no avail. When I began seeing Michael he was really in a state of regression, refusing to leave his mother's side. He had begun to refuse to defecate at all. His father wanted to simply take away the diapers and let Michael struggle with it on his own, but Michael's mother was vehement that this was too drastic. This conflict between them was certainly a key to the problem. His father was intuitively right but in most cases would react to any resistance on Michael's part with rage. Then his mother would step in and side with Michael and the father would withdraw.

Before seeing Michael I worked out a plan with his parents. His father would take the week off from his job in the city and spend it with Michael alone. Michael's mom and her other children would go into the city for the week. Then Michael's dad would let him know that the diapers stage was over. He would do this in a very positive way as someone bestowing a gift. Prior to beginning this I met with Michael a few times, so that he would have an ally in me and a place to sort out his feelings.

Michael at once struck me as a very tense, small, condensed boy. He came into my office alone but with great theatrics. His mother had to stay on the porch outside my office. Michael had to check on her every five minutes to make certain she hadn't left. He even took her car keys so she wouldn't slip away. He was very much like a little emperor in his whole manner. It would have been humorous if the price it was costing Michael were not so dear. The tragic potential in this power struggle was obvious. But there was actually a touch of humor to Michael's actions, almost a smile on his face as he ordered his mother around, which made me think he was indeed ready to grow. I suggested we tie a string to her leg so she couldn't roam too far and this made him laugh and loosen up a bit.

Once inside Michael enjoyed playing immensely. His own "greatness" was emphasized in everything he did. He became "Michael the Great" when he fought with me. His heroes in the sand were very large and elevated, out of proportion to the scene and the other figures. At one point while fighting with me he asked out of the blue, "Do you know any other boys who are shy about being naked in front of their mothers?" Michael's question not only reflected how overwhelmed he was by the intensity of his relationship with his mom and the infantile level he was stuck at, but also implied that he trusted me enough to ask for guidance. He was seeking a doorway out of his dilemma, a way to lose the struggle gracefully. We had made a positive connection that would be needed in the weeks to come.

Michael's father began his week alone with him with great success. The first five days went great, until on the sixth Michael's mother returned and everything fell apart quickly. Without diapers Michael simply refused to have bowel movements after his mother returned. Things briefly became polarized in the usual way with Michael's father becoming enraged and his mother stepping in between.

After a few days Michael began to use the toilet, replacing his diapers with anger. He was now outwardly furious at his mother, and alternatively at his father. The "no" was now being expressed outwardly through his anger rather than his bowels. His parents welcomed this with my help as a big step towards health. After three weeks Michael began to make peace with them and continued to use the toilet, unable to quite recall that it had ever been an issue.

During this period of three to four weeks, Michael came to play with me two and even three times a week. His sessions went through various phases. The sandbox was the initial focal point but could not contain all the dramas being acted out. We had to use the floor and the entire space. The "great" heroes started losing their battles and no attempts to help them were successful.

The pivotal session came on a day when Michael was resistant to entering my office. He stood with his mother on my office porch, torn between coming in with me and regressing once again. His mother scooped him up in her arms and with a sign from me passed him into my arms. This was done very gently and the whimpering which came out of Michael as I carried him was a mixture of sadness and gratitude. Without knowing why, I mentioned that we might build a labyrinth out of blocks once he was inside. This tipped the scales and he was suddenly quite willing to come in. Once inside he said to me, "But Dennis, what is a labyrinth?" Perhaps the word had some mystic archetypal power. Perhaps he was looking for any excuse to aggress rather than regress. Regardless, once inside, Michael was very intrigued and eager to begin.

Together we created an intricate labyrinth out of blocks that contained many bad guys. Two figures were designated as heroes, one his and one mine, and we entered the labyrinth and fought our way to a treasure. Here too his hero was losing despite any attempts to help him. Eventually he was killed and despite Michael's orchestrating this he looked truly sad and defeated. At this point I told him that I knew what was going on at home. (He was not aware until then that I knew.) I told him that to win this battle he had to lose, had to give up the stance he had taken. He understood what I meant and seemed very relieved to hear this.

In our next session, when the hero got trapped he allowed me to help him get free. It was at this point that Michael began to use the toilet without any fuss or anger. After this Michael developed a great fascination for superhero/arch enemy cards. He spent one whole session having me read aloud to him the qualities of each hero, listed on the back of the cards. He was no longer "Michael the Great" but was rather deferring this greatness on the heroes.

Michael moved back to the city for the school year and continued to grow and be successful with his life. He had become a relaxed, more agreeable child. His parents, with a small amount of counseling from me and the success of having helped me to help Michael, began to communicate and parent in a more balanced manner.

To become upright from crawling, stand on our own two feet and begin to walk towards what we want and away from what we don't want, we need the freedom to express the negative without loss of parental love and acceptance. We also need the firm boundaries of a parental "no" at times. A healthy yes can come only out of this. When we can express the no or surrender the no, as in Michael's case, then yes is a truly beautiful word.

In James Joyce's *Ulysses* the central female character of Molly Bloom utters a soliloquy which is one of the most beautiful in all of literature:

> And then I asked him with my eyes to ask again yes and then he asked
> me would I yes to say yes my mountain flower and first I put my arms
> around him yes and drew him down to me so he could feel my breasts

all perfume yes and his heart was going like mad and yes I said yes I will yes. (Joyce 1986, p.608)

With each yes Molly affirms herself, her sexuality, her bodily functions, her separateness and her capacity to give herself to another, and she affirms life itself in doing so. She is so obviously a character who can also say no, a self-possessed woman who pushes away what she doesn't want and opens herself to what she does want.

Most of the children I have worked with have not been able to push away what they don't want and/or push everything away regardless of what they do want. They may have been overwhelmed by a parental or environmental situation and their own emotions as well. Or it might be their own neurology that renders a healthy yes impossible, that keeps them rigidly stuck in no, making it unhealthy rather than the natural identity definer that it is meant to serve as. Often the desire to push away has become buried and forgotten, or the longing to soften and reach out to another is thwarted.

The question that arises then is how to foster a healthy no in therapy. If we recall the dream of the young man in this book's Introduction, in which something huge and monstrous dwelt in the next room, we can now see that huge monster as a personification of no, along with all the buried memories and feelings and impulses which have gone into creating it.

To draw oneself as a monster is at least to begin to open the door. The aggression that naturally arises out of symbolic play is another step towards embodying the no. There are numerous movements that express opposition, such as pounding, kicking, throwing, crashing into, etc. These may arise spontaneously or can be introduced by the therapist. When children hurl themselves at me from across the room while I hold a pillow to buffer the impact, they are not only discharging tension and expressing rage but also defining themselves. They are expressing the no and also the yes: "Yes, this is me." "Yes, I will push against you."

Affirming the negative is at the basis of all my therapeutic work with children. In every child I have worked with, unexpressed, unheard, and unresolved negative feelings are at the root of their problems. If there is one constant thread through all the play sessions I have engaged in with children it is the recognition and expression of the negative. Often this is done with a great deal of humor and even delight, so that the intensity of the feelings of rage or terror being processed may be disguised. The child still experiences the discharge but is not afraid of it.

A child cannot truly love another, a parent or friend, if they hate themselves and life in general. And they cannot stop feeling the hate until someone, another or even they themselves accepts its presence in them. My acceptance of it involves engaging the negative feelings and moving them. It is not a passive acceptance, and this is an important component. Turning the hatred outwards in a safe and sheltered space has a powerful, deeply positive effect on the child.

In Lowen's book *Pleasure*, he begins the chapter entitled "Self-awareness and Self-assertion" with the following statement:

> A person cannot be aware of his individuality unless he has the right and the ability to assert his individuality. Simply stated, self-awareness depends on self-assertion. Asserting oneself implies the idea of opposition, and it differs in this respect from expressing oneself, which doesn't have this implication. Self-assertion is a declaration of one's individuality in the face of forces which deny it. (Lowen 1970, p.147)

Looking at children's play sessions in light of this information we see the child creating a symbolic expression which contains energy and which is of the self. They then use the energy to assert themselves, thereby affirming the self. This is the basis of dynamic psychotherapy with children. We can't make it happen but can create an environment and a relationship in which it may and usually does emerge. We can assist the process by suggesting play activities or bodily movements which will provoke the process, either intuitively or with a conscious awareness of what is needed.

Self-assertion is not to be mistaken for the neurotic self-absorption that plagues so many people. A little girl made up the following story, which I have cherished ever since:

The Silly Prince

Once there was a silly prince who loved to suck on his toes. He loved doing this more than anything else in the world. As he got older he decided he should get married, as he was feeling a bit lonely. So he had all the eligible women in the kingdom brought before him. One of these women was very pretty and very smart, and the prince fell madly in love with her. "I want her!" he announced to his royal parents, the king and queen.

But his constant toe sucking disgusted this young woman. "I will not marry you unless you stop sucking your toes!" she said. The prince was horrified. "I can't stop sucking my toes!" So the woman walked off and the prince was left alone. And he did not live happily ever after.

I love this story with its deep wisdom. The prince's stubborn refusal to give up something should not be confused with the healthy self-assertion to which Lowen refers. This is not aggression but regression. Every time we take a step forward we relinquish the ground where we previously stood. The prince's problem is a common one, especially among males, often manifesting itself in later adolescence or adult life. The prince couldn't say no to his own impulses, which left him in the same weakened state as someone who can't say no to others.

What I often observe in children is how health and aliveness coexist with the beginnings of a serious neurotic disturbance. Despite all the conditioning, bad habits and thwarted energy that even very young children already manifest, there is still usually present a visible and palpable vibrancy. Even the most pacified, withdrawn child may reveal a twinkle in their eye or a mischievous smile, especially when we offer them the opportunity to play. We address this twinkle and encourage it to expand when we give the child permission to express negativity in a playful but genuine way.

I often remind myself of D.W. Winnicott's statement that "it is in playing and only in playing that the individual is able to be creative...and it is only in being creative that the individual discovers the self" (Winnicott 1971, p.54). Children are able, through play, to make enormous leaps towards health.

Chapter 6

# Falling and Leaping

Falling and leaping are two phenomena I look for and anticipate in my work with children. The energy of the playful leap is much like the energy of the playful fall. Both involve a surrendering of conscious control. In his book *Toys and Reasons* Erik Erikson cites Plato's *Laws* as providing the best formulation of play:

> He sees the model of true playfulness in the need of all young creatures, animals and human, to leap. To truly leap you must learn how to use the ground as a springboard, and how to land resiliently and safely. It means to test the leeway allowed by given limits, to outdo and yet not escape gravity. Thus, wherever playfulness prevails there is always a surprising element, surpassing mere repetition and habituation, and at its best suggesting some virgin chance conquered, some divine leeway shared. Where this "happens" it is easily perceived and acknowledged. (Erikson 1977, p.17)

A real leap ends in a fall, as described above by Erikson. Sometimes when it is a therapeutic fall, as in the case of James who "slipped on ice," the coming upright after falling feels like a leap. The two seemingly opposite directional movements are potentially the same and often apparent in the pivotal moments of a child's play therapy. The leaping/falling quality of play highlights therapeutic work with children and reflects the growth they are making. We can see it demonstrated in the leap from symbolic to physical and aggressive expression as described in previous pages, or the fall from stasis into action also seen here.

In many cases there is a leaping/falling moment that truly reflects a resolution of the underlying conflict and a firm establishment or re-establishment of a sense of self. It is indeed a perceptible thing, as are the many little leaps that often come before it. It usually feels as if some great floodgate has been opened with a huge surging forward of energy and emotion. Something new appears in the child, in their eyes and posture, in their whole demeanor that we recognize not only as wonderful but also as truly them.

When I was in supervision with Dr. Alexander Lowen in the early 1980s, his interest in my work with children centered on their body movement. "Just tell me how they move!" he would say emphatically when I would attempt to present a child by focusing on pathology or diagnosis. This insistence on what was happening not simply on a bodily level but in regards to the visible flow of energy in them was very helpful. It was then that I began to notice things such as leaping and falling, although in revisiting old cases these phenomena had often been there without me seeing them as such.

The leaping or falling may be subtle. A child may, after several sessions of describing someone stuck beneath a mountain of sand, create a scene in which dozens of wild horses pour out of an archway. In this case we can see the leap in the liberating contrast of the scene's content. We can also sense the leap in the child's demeanor and bearing. The child will then go on to demonstrate their newfound strength, perhaps by challenging me to a battle or spontaneously dancing. This act of aggression and expression will further affirm and solidify what emerged in the leap or the fall.

An oppositional child may tell a story or create a scene in which the hero dies. The same energetic quality of release, the same sense of newness and revitalization, will be present. In *Sand Play* Dora Kalff emphasizes:

> The manifestation of the self, this inner order, this pattern for wholeness, is the most important moment in the development of the person. The therapeutic relationship allows the child's self the possibility of constellating and manifesting itself. Within a free and sheltered space with the therapist serving as guardian a transformation of psychic energy can occur. (Kalff 1980, p.29)

Both falling and leaping have much in common with cathartic play but are more than mere catharsis, often happening at the same time or within the context of it, but it is often a slightly different energetic phenomenon. The leap that I am talking about is the child's spirit surfacing, expressing either a return to an integrated and safe sense of self or a first experience of it. Something new is present, like a butterfly emerging from a chrysalis. Unlike catharsis, it has a quality of joy.

The following case further illustrates the leaping aspect of children's therapy. Six-year-old Steven was referred by his school as a result of negative and erratic behavior that was requiring one-to-one attention. Steven would scream, hide, run off, refuse to participate and react as if others were attacking him without provocation. He had no friends and no social skills. He had also developed a habit of blinking his eyes repeatedly.

His parents described Steven as having a history of such behavior in the other school and day-care situations he had been in. He had been diagnosed with attention deficit disorder (ADD), but it seemed that his behavior was more emotionally based to me. As his parents were unwilling to use medication, therapy was the only option.

Steven's father was a very angry man, almost to the point of violence. In his own childhood his relationship with his father was one of bitterness. Nothing he had done ever pleased his father; nothing elicited a word of praise, let alone love. He had succeeded as an adult in running a huge corporation, which had been very successful and profitable. But all this success, because it didn't assuage his childhood wounds, only served to make him more bitter. Although none of his anger and frustration was directly about his family, as the eldest son with a very different personality from that of his father, Steven often got the brunt of his father's anger. Steven's mother used our first meeting to vent her own frustrations at her husband's moods and behavior. They agreed to come together and work on this, which they went on to do successfully.

In my first meeting with Steven I was concerned that he might indeed have a serious neurological disorder. His body movements were extremely awkward and erratic (as his behavior had been described). There was a drunken quality to his movements and to his speech as well. He began our first meeting by creating a monster named "Scuba Man." Scuba Man was a wild, amorphous creature with scuba diving gear on, who lived under the water.

On his first visit Steven also created the following scene: A large castle stood on a hillside. Below it a cemetery spread out in which "all the knights were buried." While creating the scene Steven confided that he loved cemeteries, especially old ones. He would often look for them from the car as they drove places. They calmed him and kept something alive and intact in him as well. On these family drives it must be added that his father was often raging. The escape into the solace of the cemetery took on a different note within this context.

After making the scene Steven used the encounter bats with me, obviously enjoying himself but quite concerned that I might actually hurt him. His aim, however, was quite off due to his awkward way of moving described earlier.

On Steven's next visit he created the same sand scene but with a more elaborate cemetery, with flags and statues. This time he actually buried knights under each gravestone. The cemetery theme continued to become more elaborate over the next few visits. He also insisted on recreating his monster Scuba Man during each visit, and these too became more elaborate with breathing hoses and water guns. These were more defined and quite sophisticated for a six-year-old, not only in concept but also in the execution of them.

Steven began taking great pleasure in hitting the mattress with a tennis racket. This too became a ritualistic part of each visit. During one bout of hitting he began to talk about how frightening and how infuriating his father was. Meanwhile I had met with his father to encourage/insist that he deal with his rage rather than subject his children to it.

A breakthrough, a leaping, came in Steven's sixth visit. I suggested that he make up a story about a cemetery which I would write down, something I often do with children. Steven had me close my eyes as he hid something in the sand. When I opened them he had placed one gravestone in the sand. Then he began to tell me the story. It was really the same story of his previous scenes, in which knights had been slain in battle and were buried. But there was some new tension and excitement. He talked slowly and kept me in suspense for quite some time as he described each grave. Then finally as he was describing one particular grave, it immediately opened up and a huge monster came out, destroying everyone. Unlike his monster drawings, which had a comical quality, this creature was very primal. Although the actions of the monster would make it seem purely cathartic, the quality of it was also joyful.

I suggested that he might act like the monster with me or towards me, at which point he began to attack me with an encounter bat. What was striking in Steven's attack was the absence of awkwardness. The "drunken" quality to his movements was gone, replaced by an almost graceful quality. What I had originally suspected might be an organic problem had been fear – fear of his father and fear of his own pent-up anger at his father personified by the buried monster. When the monster leapt up out of its grave, so too did Steven's own sense of power. He even began standing up to his father on occasions after this visit, which his father tolerated and perhaps secretly admired. He began his own treatment probably as a result of the shift in dynamics that his son's leaping had helped bring about.

Steven's next session began with a scene in which the knights, now alive, battled each other. The cemetery was gone and remained gone. The battling between the knights reflected the normal competitiveness and combativeness that boys his age engage in. This time in Steven's Scuba Man drawing he had shed his scuba gear and come up on to land. He proceeded to describe how Scuba Man "pissed on his mother and father." He did so with great laughter, and told his mother about it when she came to pick him up. Was he marking his territory the way many animals do? Was he punishing them but also playing with them? I am not sure, but meanwhile Steven had become much more social in school. His teacher saw none of the behaviors that had brought him to therapy in the first place. Steven's aggression at this point, expressed in the combativeness of the knights and the urinating monster, was healthier and more balanced.

Steven's leap occurred when his monster leapt up out of its grave. This corresponded to his moving in a new and integrated way. It also coincided with his speaking up for himself at home and with his Scuba Man emerging from the sea. This was like one large, rapid evolution. In particular, Steven's Scuba Man paralleled his own ego development.

In Steven's early sessions what was particularly striking was a way he had of moving when he became energized which was like a bucking motion. It seemed as if his whole organism was trying to respond to the energy it experienced in a normal way. Yet he was being thwarted in his efforts and it came out instead as a sort of half-leap. It is helpful to look at all the children we work with as "trying to be normal" but unable to succeed on their own.

Energetically, what happens when we leap is that our body actually "lets down" in order to accomplish it. Our breathing and our center of gravity actually deepen. When the leaping is visible and palpable, as it was with Steven, it is a truly numinous experience. With the child the experience is expressed via play rather than through a spoken realization, as it would be with an adult. With an adult the articulation of the experience helps to root it and affirm it in our consciousness. In this way the words are an important part of such a pivotal experience. With a child it is often not necessary that there be a verbal acknowledgment of the leap and all its ramifications. The child affirms it by playing and interacting and being in a new way. Yet it is as powerful as the equivalent experience in the adult, as if a great burden has finally been lifted, a long sought for answer has been given. In many ways it is more monumental because it may spare the child years of internal struggle and pain. The following case is a wonderful example of the leaping moment.

Six-year-old Katy was brought for therapy after barely surviving a three-year-long divorce and custody battle between her parents. Her parents often used Katy, their only child, as a weapon in this vicious battle. Neither parent recognized his or her own part in Katy's ensuing unhappiness. Each was quick to point out the other's mistakes, often quite correctly. Her mother was often impatient and self-absorbed. Her father used Katy as a crutch, having her sleep with him at night to comfort him until he met another woman.

This overwhelmed her as well as sexually charging her organism. Many parents refuse to accept that their children can be sexually stimulated when forced to sleep with them or bathe with them after a certain age. When I ask them at what age it will become inappropriate to do so they are vague, but they often start to be more aware of their child as a separate person because of this question. In the 1970s, when every other boy I worked with had been labeled "hyperactive," I discovered that most of these boys lived alone with their mothers and slept with them at night, again for the mother's sake. Though their mothers were not molesting these boys, they were being sexually stimulated in a subliminal way. The result was an overwhelmed and agitated child. Removing the child from the mother's bed immediately brought about a change in the boy's behavior.

In Katy's case it simply fueled her misery, making the capacity for her needs to be met impossible. Katy had deteriorated in school, unable to do even the minimal amount of work. She seemed desperate for attention, especially from boys. Her whole demeanor reflected the misery she felt. By the time I met with Katy her parents were so concerned about her that they were willing to recognize their mistakes. They went on not only to acknowledge the remorse they needed to feel but also to begin to mend their ways.

Katy entered my play space with the weight of the world on her small shoulders. Her face was a mask of pain. She was not fearful to be alone with me, but was fearful of the monster drawings on my wall. This is very unusual. She found the sandbox a refuge and went on to create a scene in which her father was being drowned in the sea "for being so mean." After doing this she seemed already less fearful and quite pleased with this act. Later on her mother was also placed in the sea and drowned.

Katy was quite eager to return at the end of our visit to pursue this theme of punishing her parents. In the following sessions she continued to develop the scene and expanded it into the space. She found many ways of destroying her parents, but came to prefer making them out of clay and chopping them up or tearing them to pieces. Meanwhile her parents reported a much happier child at home and a more responsive child in school.

During one subsequent visit Katy began to play "Follow the Leader," dancing around the room and encouraging me to follow her. She was quite surprised when I followed her lead, unused as she was to adults paying attention to her unless they wanted something from her. What began as her enjoying bossing me around ended in an upbeat and playful dance process. At one point Katy decided she wanted to bounce. She tried doing so on my mattress but couldn't get as high as she wanted. She dragged out a small trampoline that I keep in my office for such occasions and began to jump on it.

While Katy jumped I kept time on a drum. She began to sing as she jumped and although the singing began with angry proclamations, it became infused with joy. At first she sang, "I hate my dad" and then "I hate my mom." This evolved rather quickly into "I love to jump," then "I love the sea," "I love the mountains," "I love the wind," "I love the sun and the sun loves me." This last phrase about the sun was repeated over and over again. As she sang about the sun, sunlight came pouring in through the windows. (It had been a cloudy day up until that point.) I was awestruck but Katy took it as a matter of course. She saw my reaction to the sunlight and sang "The sun is my friend," and then "I love my life, I love my life," over and over again.

It was as if all the many particles that make up a life came together in her dance and leapt towards the heavens in Katy's triumphant moment, a moment of synchronicity. Her invocation of the four elements – earth, water, air and fire – was experienced by Katy as joyful but also as very matter of fact. When the child becomes whole again they seem to take it in their stride, as if to say "This is how life is supposed to be," which of course it is.

Katy would still have to go home and live with fairly narcissistic parents. Life would not be suddenly so easy, but she was more there within herself. Ordering me around helped her to feel empowered, emboldened. I suspected she would be more demanding at home and less used by her parents as a result, which was what happened. Proclaiming her right to love her life, in the wake of much negative discharge, awakened something in her that I believe would stay awake.

Although leaping and falling have much in common with the cathartic play referred to by Erik Erikson, they are more than simple catharsis. When present in a child's play, it is a sign that the cathartic work done thus far is having the desired effect of freeing the child; freeing them to move and think and express themselves in a new way.

Lowen's idea that children's play must show movement in some small or large way is a great guide to use. It need not be as dramatic as the two children described here, but it will often have the sense of a leap or a fall, if we are open to this. It may appear in their sandplay rather than out in space. How we recognize it is by being present enough that we too are moved by it. It is not an intellectual experience for either child or therapist. We need not be dragged down onto the floor on the slippery ice, although that is certainly a thrilling way of co-experiencing the fall/leap.

I believe that children sense what we know, what we believe. I think they will also hold back to spare us discomfort. As a result, we as therapists must keep working on ourselves, seeking and making peace with our monsters, attempting to free up thwarted energies in ourselves through our own falling and leaping, being open to the bigness of life that children live so close to.

Children are usually not so identified with their defense systems, and this allows them to let go of them or to restructure them into a more functional form. This is really what therapy with children is all about, the restructuring of form via dynamic play.

Chapter 7

# Interlude with Monsters

Cuchulainn, the great hero of Irish legends, was famous not only for his bravery but also for his "warp spasm." This transformation happened to him when he prepared for battle and is similar to what I encourage children to do as we begin to work together. Cuchalainn doesn't live in this form. He becomes it to protect, to avenge and to restore balance.

> The first warp spasm seized Cuchulainn, and made him into a monstrous thing, hideous and shapeless, unheard of. His shanks and his joints, every knuckle and angle and organ from head to foot, shook like a tree in the flood or a reed in the stream. His body made a furious twist inside his skin, so that his feet and shins and knees twitched to the rear and his heels and calves switched to the front.
>
> The balled sinews of his calves switched to the front of his shins... His face and features became a red bowl. He sucked one eye so deep into his head that a wild crane couldn't probe it into his cheek out of the depths of his skull: the other eye fell out along his cheek. His mouth weirdly distorted... His heart boomed loud in his breast like the baying of a watchdog at its feed or the sound of a lion among bears.
>
> Malignant mists and spurts of fire the torches of Badb flickered in red in the vaporous clouds that rose boiling above his head, so fierce was his fury. The hair of his head twisted like the tangle of a red thornbush stuck in a gap; if a royal apple tree with all its kingly fruit were shaken above him, scarce an apple would reach the ground but each would be spiked on a bristle of his hair as it stood up on his scalp with rage.
>
> The hero-halo rose out of his brow, long and broad as a warrior's whetstone, long as a snout and he went mad rattling his shields, urging on his charioteer and harassing the hosts. Then, tall and thick, steady and strong, high as the mast of a noble ship, rose from the dead center of his skull a straight spout of black blood darkly and magically smoking like the smoke from a royal hostel when a king is coming to be cared for at the close of a winter day. (Smith 2007)

An in-depth approach to therapy attempts to do the same with the child's defense system, their sense of integrity and their developing ego. The paradox of Cuchalainn's monster is that it is hideous and yet a "hero-halo rises out of it." Children's monster drawings always embody this same paradox. There is an underlying nobility of purpose that is felt in the creation of them but that doesn't translate well in images of these drawings.

My life has been cluttered and filled with monsters for many years. The walls of my office are overflowing with these monstrous forms. I see them in the offices of other therapists who have studied with me and I hear about other methods of monster use that are derivatives of my original impulse or someone else's awareness and appreciation of these primary forms we create from early on (Figure 7.1).

Figure 7.1 A variety of monsters

I have read that the Buddhist saint Milarepa, while sitting in a mountain cave in deep meditation, suddenly heard a group of demons at the entrance to the cave clamoring to come in. They threatened and shrieked but Milarepa calmly invited them to come in and take tea with him. I have been inviting other people's demons to come and play in my office for over 30 years, and have on occasion actually made tea for them. Like Max in Maurice Sendak's *Where the Wild Things Are* (1963), Milarepa and his demons could coexist. This is also true of children, who live in a state not so dissimilar to an enlightened one.

Some children use monster drawing as an ongoing means of expressing and exploring and changing in the exaggerated form that the monster allows. I urge some children to draw one periodically so I can see what has happened to their relationship with the monster and the sense of self it so often reflects. I have shown some children and even parents the evolution that the child's monsters have gone through as evidence that things are indeed different. One child almost only drew monsters, and these took the form of a dialogue with me about himself. Although his monsters were fierce they were offered to me with great tenderness. As they rapidly evolved, so did he. We spoke mainly as it pertained to his monsters and almost never about his life situation, but as his monsters became more articulate so too did he in the rest of his life. As they took on more complex forms, diversifying and expanding their movement repertoire, he too became cognitively more versatile and socially more flexible and self-possessed.

I have never had a child have an adverse reaction to drawing themselves as monsters, but then I do exercise certain caution. I would not encourage a child to draw a monster if they were actively psychotic. I would also not encourage this if a child were in the early phase of trauma recovery. Although most children will modify the size, aspects and intensity of the monster form based on what they can handle, I am aware and sensitive to a child's defense system and what state it is in. That said, however, for a child who has experienced abuse the monster can express the experience on a bodily level in a way that might otherwise be inexpressible. One such child made monsters that oozed and spewed and erupted toxins from every part of their bodies. What started out as expressions of what the abuse felt like ended up being the very weapon her monsters used to attack and ultimately avenge the abuse (Figure 7.2).

Sometimes the monster drawings that fill my walls begin to have a life of their own, separate from me. They evolve, they interact with each other through the various children who drew them, and they inspire each other as

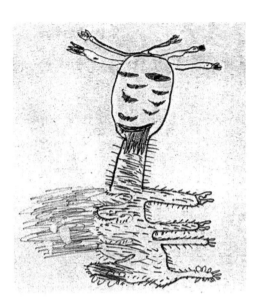

*Figure 7.2 A sexually abused eight-year-old girl's first monster exuding toxins as weapons*

well as the children. They battle with each other and sometimes even fall in love with each other. This community of monsters has great humor to it. Unlike the monsters we run from or dread as small children that lurk in the shadows of our room and our consciousness, these monsters, perhaps because they are shared with me and with an ongoing host of other children, are not so frightening. Even the bloodiest and/or hungriest of them doesn't ever elicit the same sense of dread. I believe that the act of sharing and in a sense humanizing these monsters makes them more familiar without losing any of their power. They are after all, or must become if we are to be healthy, a part of our humanity.

Five-year-old Thomas initially refused to draw a monster as he was afraid it would not be as good as the others he saw on the walls of my office. Struggling with a learning disability and the perfectionism that I find so often accompanies this, he was unwilling to risk not getting it right. He understood intuitively that what he drew didn't look anything like what he imagined he would draw. But he longed to join the community of monsters, so he discovered that if he drew an invisible monster but gave it a name he could avoid any self-criticism or the imagined judgment from others. As his was the only invisible monster on my wall he had actually made something unique. He dubbed his monster "Zambu" and after a while drew some clothing for him on the reverse side of the picture so no one could see. His monster's clothes were drawn with the lopsided quality that I find is typical of many dyslexic children's early drawings.

A few other children, intrigued by his idea, drew invisible monsters after this and this unsocial child, referred for therapy because of this, began to socialize in a sense with these other children through his monster and its invisibleness. Many weeks later, after much growth, Thomas went back and let me flip his drawing over so that Zambu's clothing was revealed. This slow emerging into visibility had a sweetness to it and it honored his sense of integrity as an approach to the seemingly simple act of monster drawing. He went on later in that same session to draw a series of visible monsters, discovering that by drawing monsters whose very nature allowed for a distortion of form he was less inhibited and actually drew some very interesting ones. One monster actually had the skeletons of people it had eaten inside one of its many bellies. It was as if Thomas was discovering form as he was playing with it, discovering the joy of giving form to his very fine imagination. Rather than feeling exposed he felt seen and wanted to.

Daniel, a child whose parents' very prolonged and bitter divorce had rendered him quite battered, drew a monster named "Thing" who "scared the poop out of parents that were fighting." This monster not only satisfied something in Daniel and helped alert his father to the need to silence his too vocal anger at his ex-wife, but also inspired many other children as well who were going through similar divorce battles. Many of these children dragged their parents in after sessions to show them Thing and point out his parent-censoring function. Many children took comfort not only in the idea of this monster who had the power to stop such parental battles, but also in the realization that other children suffered the same experience.

Eight-year-old Rebecca was involved in a very nasty tug of war between a narcissistic, cold mother and a well-meaning but rigid father, with a very nasty older brother thrown in the picture as well. She drew herself first as "Three Boobs," a female warrior monster that slew older brothers (Figure 7.3). Then, after a few cathartic sessions in which she came to feel more empowered, she drew herself as "Thousand Boobs," more fertility goddess than warrior but just as capable of destroying older brothers. Her multi-breasted beasts seemed like an apt form for her to take, as they addressed her need for maternal nurturance and her outrage at her brother's bullying. Her thousand-boobed monster was similar to a famous image of the goddess Artemis, a kindred spirit of this very powerful girl (Figure 7.4). Her monsters inspired others with their comical yet mythological quality. They had a deep

*Figure 7.3 "Three Boobs"*

1,000   BooBs

*Figure 7.4 "Thousand Boobs"*

therapeutic power for her. She felt very satisfied mounting them on my wall and knowing that others would see them, including her older brother, who was very shocked by them. I do think he treated her with more respect after this, in part wowed by the feminine power of all those breasts and also because he knew I was now involved in the family picture.

Among all the "Fangs" and "Spikes" and "Killers" who have dotted my walls, there has also been "Big Nose" and eventually "The Big Nose Family." There have been dragons of every size and color. There was "No Name" and "Son of No Name" and "Brother of No Name," all drawn by different children inspired by each other. These monsters have run the gamut from tiny to huge, from amorphous to very defined, from unrecognizable as anything to almost human, or barely monstrous. Many spoke directly about the child's emotional state at the onset of therapy, such as "Bloody Pulp" who was a graphic depiction of how this divorce-beaten child felt inside. One sexually abused child drew monsters that exuded noxious substances from every pore of their bodies as she herself began the process of ridding her body of the abusive experience. The bigness of life that these monsters personify is endless and so are the ways in which children envision it. The paradox of being able to express serious and even tragic sentiments within the same image as humor and delight is unique to children and perhaps enlightened adults (Figure 7.5).

## The mythic

Children love myths. "Once upon a time..." or "Once there lived..." hooks in even the most jaded of children with its possibility of story. There is a deep urge for story even if there is also a resistance to it these days due to the passive video game playing mind set that so many children have thrust on them from early on. But story does still win out if we encourage it. Many myths possess the violence that most video games are all about, yet there is often a teaching inherent in myth as well as the possibility of redemption.

There is often a mythological quality to children's monsters. Most of these monsters act like gods and goddesses, and are certainly godlike in their stature and power. Like the chthonic gods of the ancient Greeks, such as the Titans or Poseidon, or those of India such as Shiva, these figures create, destroy and often sustain life. They are prone to fits of jealousy and revenge, like humans, and are capable of avenging these feelings in an over-the-top fashion. They hurl lightning bolts or tridents to destroy entire villages, or they leave heroes such as Odysseus floating in the sea for several days having destroyed their ships. But they also create healing springs with the very same weapon. They provoke change by forcing it upon the heroes or heroines of the mythic stories they appear in. This is perhaps their real underlying power and lure. They force change and in doing so make things happen, make life happen.

*Figure 7.5 More monsters*

Poseidon is one of the gods most like the monsters that children draw, with his great form-altering powers. He sends earthquakes, volcanic eruptions and tsunamis. He upsets everything but allows for transformation because of this. The word transformation means the total change of a form, as if by magic:

> Transformation is the essence of the journey into the unconscious and of the extension of man beyond the mundane reality of his narrow life.

The instinct that drives us to constant change and transformation, however great the dangers and powerful the monsters we encounter along the way, is the instinct that Poseidon personifies – the instinct that drives us to wander through endless adventures, as Odysseus was forced to do by the sea god, until we reach Ithaca, the place where we started from, and, through transformed eyes, see it again for the first time. (Stassinopoulos 1983, p.47)

In play therapy, children play the role of Poseidon both in his wrathful and also in his spring opening capacity. But they are also identified with the hero, needing to negotiate with the angry god. Play, like Poseidon, has the ability to upset the old balance in the service of growth. Children naturally push the boundaries of a play material to see how far they can do so. They build block towers higher and higher, knowing that they will come crashing down, but learning how to negotiate balance in the process. It is one of the innate paradoxes of play.

## The Messed Up Monster Game

I have invented many games involving monsters over the years for children, often with their help, that involve monsters. Some of these games were designed to help them tolerate form changing. One of these was invented originally for a dyslexic child who was such a perfectionist that he couldn't let himself enjoy anything for fear the form wouldn't look the way he intended it to. So I made up a drawing game in which the person drawing a monster is "messed up" by the other person several times while trying to do so. The paper can be knocked or pulled out from under them. Their arm can be yanked on or jiggled. The "mess" that results is then turned into a monster by the person who was drawing it, by adding as many lines as needed but without the erasure of any lines. The monsters that this technique produces are really quite wonderful: very wild and odd and organic. The perfectionist relaxes. The inhibited child lets go. The monster and all its inherent vitality win out. This game can be very physical, very aggressive and is always great fun.

## The Cheating Game

Another game I invented is called the "Cheating Game" and I made it with the help of a very oppositional boy who always had to win at everything or he would throw a huge fit. In this game, one of the rules is that you must cheat in order to win. The game does have rules of course in order to make cheating a possibility. The rules may vary but are simply that each person draws three monsters on the designated side of their piece of paper and then attacks the other person's monsters one at a time, destroying a limb or a head or an appendage. Then it is the other person's turn. Of course one can make many monsters as cheating is acceptable, so you could make ten or even a hundred. When it is your turn you can destroy all of a monster or several at once or the entire side. But then your partner can inform you that there are numerous invisible monsters on their side waiting to attack. This becomes terribly inventive and rather silly but even the most oppositional child joins in and accepts the seemingly ruleless rules. It can go on endlessly which disorganizes the idea of winning so inherent in certain children. Again, this paradoxically corrects the problem at least during the play. Even the child most concerned with winning gives in to the cheating and this becomes more important than victory. Children emerge from this game flush faced and triumphant, even though it is often unclear who won.

I think that in the case of both the Messed Up Monster Game and the Cheating Game the use of the monster as the form is central. The personal is transcended. The old rules of conduct, whether they are perfectionism, the need to win, or fear of aggressing, are momentarily forgotten. The child senses they have already stepped into unknown territory where they may act differently, letting go of their own rules and inflexibility, becoming open to finding a new way.

## Clay monster battles

One other game that is immensely popular with children and used throughout their therapy is the clay monster battle. This involves each of us making a monster out of clay, roughly four inches to eight inches in length. These monsters need not be elaborate for they are destroyed rather quickly in the throws of battle. I designate a ring for fighting in on a piece of paper or cardboard and each of our monsters takes a corner, just as in a real boxing or wrestling match. After I "ding" a gong three times the monsters come in slugging and continue to do so until the gong dings again. Children are usually cautious at first as to how hard they can hit my monster. I calculate how hard I attack based on the child. I may need to model playful aggression or provoke it. I may need to hold back so they can emerge. Heads and limbs fly, bodies are smashed and a certain amount of cheating goes on despite this not being the Cheating Game. All in all it results in very dirty hands, lots of laughs and much aggressive discharge. I find girls enjoy this game the most.

And the possibility is there with clay that the end result of our intermingled monster mess could be reshaped into something creative, something even beautiful.

Sometimes the battles have a real emotional intensity to them. They are not just play. The girl mentioned in Chapter 1 who made a multi-tiered fountain out of clay as her father lay dying of Aids did so out of a monster battle. Her angry discharge brought up tears that in turn brought up the fountain image from her unconscious. It served her well as a beacon of her own strength and her love for her father as he withered into death in the subsequent months, but it emerged out of her anger. Without her angry monster battle the fountain would not have emerged.

When I have led training workshops for other therapists, one of the more popular moments each day is a clay monster battle that begins in dyads, identical to the one described above. Then each dyad joins forces and battles another dyad. These form groups of four and battle other groups of four, depending on the number of people in attendance. In the final battle there are two large groups that each make a monster together and then battle each other with lots of shouts and applause and hissing. After this battle they all mould the clay into one group monster, with each person contributing a part. It is always a very tender moment despite or perhaps because of what transpired before. The group looks relaxed but energized. All faces are flushed and all eyes are flashing. These monstrous entertainments, as fun as they obviously are for the child to engage in, must also be seen for the real therapeutic power they possess as well. Returning to the idea of paradox, the same form that can give rise to belly laughs and a letting go of rigidity can also release deep anger and grief and thus open the heart.

Many years ago, during a particularly painful time in my own struggle to know myself better, I had the following dream:

> I am walking in an underground stone labyrinth with a young boy and it is my responsibility to guide him to safety. We enter a room and there sits an ancient monster, more human than beast, but still monstrous. I know he is very, very old and very powerful and I am repulsed and terrified by this creature, but the young boy runs and sits in his lap, unafraid and unharmed. It is the very "safety" I have been asked to lead him to, this lap of the monster. The two belong together.

Long afterwards I realized that this monster-man was the same monster that I felt the presence of behind the closed door in the dream when I was 18, he who had first awakened me to me. The child-ego was safe in his lap, the adult-ego was not. At times life seems to be an attempt at reconciling the two or actually the three: child, man and monster.

Chapter 8

# Form and Formlessness

Sandplay therapy's greatest power lies in its ability to replicate, express and contain the disintegration/reintegration process which all life goes through when normal growth and especially deep change occur. This form to formlessness to form process *is* life. We imbue, embellish and express this process via symbols and stories, adding richness and texture with our imaginations. The personal and collective unconscious speak through these rather than ordinary language. Yet each story and symbol is relevant insofar as it facilitates or attempts to describe this process of structural change or our resistance to it, which is always an essential part of the process. They facilitate and enrich the excursions into formlessness needed in order to change.

Certain symbols are particularly relevant to this fundamental process I am describing, as they express and contain the very energy needed for transformation to occur. They not only herald change, but also foster it through their mysterious relationship with the deeper Self. The snake is an excellent example of this. It is a symbol of life and death and rebirth. It was often associated with healing and was used by Hippocrates in his medical diagnosis and treatment. The snake was associated with life at its deepest, with the instinctual power and wisdom of the natural world. Within the context of the sandbox, the snake seems to be a channel for the life-affirming energy needed for change. It usually appears when something deep has risen to the surface and is accessible. It signifies that some big change could now occur if we are able to use these risen energies. The snake and other symbols of transformation appear in the sand only after the structure, the material, and the therapeutic relationship of the sandplay process have begun to stir things up.

Ultimately sandplay allows the child to express and give form to the formless intensity of life: the feelings and impulses within themselves and in the world around them. They must negotiate these on a minute-to-minute basis, usually unbeknownst to their parents and to the world around them. It is this intensity that when thwarted gives rise to the myriad problems that children develop and present to us in therapy. Herein lies the early roots of the struggles we as adults have as well.

Often other forms of play are needed. I sometimes introduce activities that directly relate to structural change. One boy recently began therapy with a high level of rigidity and defensiveness that was interfering with his life. His initial sandplay was interesting, but somewhat dead. He was a perfectionist and a know-it-all, who needed to win at everything. I engaged him in a game in which we built forts out of blocks and then smashed each other's down. This loosened him up and when he went back to the sand his play was more alive, although also more chaotic. He seemed less defended and more vulnerable due to this destructive play. In smashing my fort and letting me smash his, the defensive structure within, which was not serving him in his life, began to change as well.

All play materials that are therapeutic allow for this form-altering process to occur. Sandplay in particular allows the child to break down form into formlessness and then eventually into a more functional form. This may need to happen many times until the form is right. The box and the medium of the sand together contain and support this breaking down and reorganizing of form. It is always occurring when there is growth and change in the child. It is often visible in the sandplay process, which allows the therapist and the child to witness and experience this transformation. It is breathtaking to witness – like the birth of a child or the emergence of a butterfly from its chrysalis. The following case exemplifies this process.

Eleven-year-old David was referred for therapy due to the sudden onset of panic attacks that were occurring frequently and disrupting his life. He had always seemed to his parents and teachers to be a very happy well-adjusted child. He was smart, athletic, and a leader among his peers. No one could make sense of this sudden panic taking hold. His parents could think of no event that might have precipitated his panic other than the placement in his classroom for the second year of a very unruly boy who was "David's opposite" in every way.

David had been a very "easy" child and had not really gone through the "terrible twos." He had never really learned to say no to his parents or others. As he was entering puberty, it made sense to me that the lack of this important developmental skill would begin to have consequences; that the unexpressed "no" would appear as symptoms. His parents had felt lucky to have such an easy child, but with help they also grasped the possible connection between his lack of assertion as a toddler and this sudden anxiety. They agreed to make room for the assertive behavior that might come from David as a result of therapy; to tolerate his pushing against them in an effort to grow.

Was the wild boy in his classroom a shadow figure for him, provoking the dormant energies that David needed to bring into consciousness as he entered this stage of his growth? Or was the symptom itself his own inner directed aggression and life force calling out, expressing itself so as to be heard and found and integrated into his personality?

In my first meeting with him, David struck me as a remarkable youngster. He was unusually mature for his age in many ways; some would describe him as an "old soul." I have noticed that children such as David often have a difficult time negotiating the normal developmental stages of childhood, perhaps because on some level they are beyond them. However, this type of child still needs to struggle through these stages and will suffer if they do not.

David only worked in the sand during the entire course of his treatment. From the onset, David's scenes were unusually spiritual in nature. They were perhaps too much so, as if David was too open to this bigger, deeper level of life. In most of the scenes, the figure of Shiva was present in a central role. In David's first sand scene, Shiva was standing in the middle of a lake in the center of a town, keeping things from falling apart. David made this scene with great relish and with no awareness of its connection to his symptoms. David did not know that Shiva was the god of destruction and creation who made things fall apart in the service of growth, but he came to appreciate the unconscious choice of figures.

Due to his age and his unusual maturity, as well as the severity of his symptoms, I spoke to David more directly than I might with other children. I let him know from the beginning of therapy that I thought his problems had to do with his need to be able to say no, explaining its function as a protective filter. I urged him to practice on his parents who were ready for it. He took me up on this and began to regularly say no to his parents. At first these attempts simply made him laugh, as they were so out of character. Although these efforts at home helped, David's real transformation came through his sand scenes and his relationship with me while in the process of making them. The following is a description of David's subsequent scenes. One can see his efforts at introducing chaos, as well as the metaphysical level on which he is struggling (and the humor he includes). The introduction of aggression and playfulness can also be seen.

Scene 2: A place in which everything seems upside down. "Everything in this town is messed up and leads nowhere. Everything that should be underground is on top and vice versa. The treasures are all above ground and the people who live below must come up to see them." An icon was placed right side up in the center of the town with the statue of Shiva watching from the corner.

Scene 3: Nine deep, narrow holes are dug in the sand with cats sitting by each and a group of people sitting on the very edge of the box. "This is a world where people bring their cats to get new lives. There are nine lakes and the cats are put into one lake and come out another one reborn. Each lake fits the personality of the cat that enters it. People come to watch. It is a very peaceful place. There is a chalice in the center."

Scene 4: There are many statues of gods centered around an eye-shaped space. "This is the place where everything that is worth something is. Whatever people are searching for is here and you can only see what it is that you are after. What you are after is what you see!"

Scene 5: There is a labyrinth-like path with a guillotine at the entrance. "In this place you fall into a hole and at the very end you die. The guillotine at the start doesn't chop your head off though; it throws you to this place. It is a mysterious place. There is a sign at the very end that says "Jump!"

Scenes 6 and 7: These two scenes were a continuation and are too elaborate to describe in their entirety. In the middle of the box are a number of gods, monsters, and other creatures revolving around the god Shiva, forming a perfect mandala. On the sides there are two teams, the green and the blue, that are fighting for control. These two teams are both aggressive and comical, part gladiator and part slapstick. They are constantly knocking everything down and then some little guy comes out of a house in the corner of the scene and puts everything back again. This happens repeatedly. Things fall apart and are reassembled, again and again. The mood is cathartic but happy.

Though there was a little remaining anxiety prior to sleep, at this point David's panic attacks had ceased. Before bed he would sometimes "freak out," as he put it, and worry about his own or his parents' death, but otherwise he felt fine. David's parents wondered if he should end therapy, but it seemed to him and me that there was a bit more work to be done.

David's last two visits with me had a mythic quality. In the first, he came in and set up all of the god figures in the collection on the edge of the sandbox. He looked at me mischievously and began to talk. As he spoke he began to slowly knock the gods into the box with his body, as if by mistake. One by one they were toppled until the box was a mess of fallen gods. He was very content, almost smugly so. He had accomplished something enormous with this series of gestures. Despite the simplicity and playfulness of the act, it was deeply cathartic.

In my last session with David, he and I once more examined the months prior to the onset of his panic attacks. I had been sure that something must have helped to trigger them, beyond the underlying need for change on a basic level. David recalled in this visit that about a month prior to the beginning of the panic attacks he had fallen from a diving board at the local pool. Although he had not cut his chest deeply, the wounds looked gruesome. He may have also hit his head slightly, though no concussion was found. His mother had not been there with him as it was close to home and he had wanted to be allowed to exercise some independence.

David spoke of the shattering effect this fall had on him. He had felt different afterwards, as if he was no longer the same child or the world had suddenly changed. This sudden fall from innocence and the realization that his parents would not always be able to protect or catch him must have been pivotal for David. It is also interesting that both David and his parents had forgotten this incident in my questioning at the onset of treatment.

The concept of panic has its origins in the ideas surrounding the Greek god Pan. Pan struck terror in those who would not follow the sound of his flute; they "panicked." Those who would follow were blessed with great joy. Pan was a rustic god, the offspring of Zeus and a nymph, and was associated with animals, sexuality and the instinctual life in general. In statues and paintings of Pan his upper body is human but his lower half is depicted as that of a goat. This is the key to understanding and treating panic. If we pull away from the instinctual lower half of ourselves, it will re-emerge in the form of symptoms. To end panic we must help the individual feel more comfortable with these unacceptable parts of themselves. The sandplay process offers a means of dipping down into that lower half, exploring, and reintegrating it.

I have worked with a number of people over the years whose panic attacks began after a serious fall. Like David, the ground was fertile for the thwarted instinctual self to erupt and the fall seemed to have helped it to happen. The final outcome has always been positive, as they came to feel whole, though the process first involved a stage of disintegration.

There was a great silence after David told me about his fall on the diving board. We both realized the importance of what he had said and sat with that realization for a while. The silence was numinous. David then made what became his final scene. He told me to close my eyes and he would tell me when to open them. When I was finally allowed to open my eyes, I was surprised to find an empty sandbox. He very happily told me it was "the land of no mind, no thing, and no where." He was immensely satisfied and said he didn't need to come anymore.

Working with a child such as David is an awesome experience. He helped me to put into thoughts, words, and actions everything I had learned over the many years I have been working with people. He validated the power of sandplay to help facilitate and articulate what words alone cannot: that miraculous ability, within the context of the right setting and relationship, for the psyche to transform. David began therapy in a "fallen apart" state. Therapy helped make that falling apart a creative and life-affirming experience.

The ancient Greeks, using the myths associated with the god Dionysos, envisioned a five-part cycle of transformation. The stages of this cycle, often enacted as part of an initiation ritual, mirror the stages that we all go through to some extent as we attempt to change. These stages are: descent, dismemberment, death, rebirth and resurrection. They mirror the stages that a seed goes through as it falls to the earth, disintegrates and lies as if dead until the spring when it regenerates into plant and then bloom and fruit and begins the cycle all over again. This might seem like a rather grandiose schema to use in therapy with children, but they do indeed follow the stages in their play therapy experience if it is truly therapeutic.

Descent is experienced whenever we drop below the everyday state of consciousness, whether we do so intentionally via therapy or as a result of an internal or external life crisis. As children sit or squat by the sand and put their hands into it they experience this as a descent, into both their body and their imagination. The physical reactions I have described in previous pages, such as passing gas or having to urinate or flushing and panting, happen due to this descent into the body.

The next stage, dismemberment, happens whenever the old form falls apart. This happens quite easily for children as they are less identified with the form, less afraid of the new. What can feel shattering for the adult does not for the child. They may regress a bit in the process, even talking babytalk for a few hours or even days after a session in which this dismembering play has occurred. I try to remember to warn parents of this phenomenon so they will not be alarmed by it. David was a classic example. For all his seeming maturity, the minute his play reflected or actually fostered form falling apart, he begin to speak in a babyish voice. Most of David's play was in this dismemberment stage.

I have children erect and destroy block towers during this stage, or else make figures out of clay and demolish them. One of the most used objects in my collection is a small but functional guillotine. Many parents have been beheaded, as I have I myself on numerous occasions. Although totally unorthodox, it has been the salvation of many a child. Sometimes this dismemberment happens in a ritualistic way with great solemnity, as in a child who dealt with his mother's death by making her body out of clay, beheading it, and then anointing it with magic potions before entombing it in a crystal lined, candlelit cave. After doing this for several sessions he had made some peace with the loss.

The next stage, which the Greeks called death, is really more of a still resting place, like the still center of a storm or the place between breaths spoken of in meditation practices. When David knocked his gods into the sand, the feeling afterwards was like this – a sense of relief and quiet.

Rebirth and resurrection often happen simultaneously. Rebirth could best be described as a spark igniting or a seed germinating, with resurrection as its fire or its fruit. David's humorous yet awesome "place of no mind" was an unusual version of this. But for him it served as both stages and a fitting place to end and yet begin from. He was revitalized by his sequence of form-altering play.

Chapter 9

# Harnessing Chaos
## Helping Children with Neurological Disorders

Over the past ten years I have observed a very different type of child entering my practice in ever-increasing numbers. Today these children make up the bulk of the younger patients I work with. They present not only a different set of symptoms at the onset of treatment, but often a different way of playing. From the onset I could sense the organic nature of their problems in my interactions with them, and could also see a pattern in their play that was unique. Upon evaluation by a pediatric neurologist, these children always tested as having one of the many neurological disorders plaguing our children today. The decision to assess them for these disorders was often based on a pattern of play or the use of their bodies in their play and in general. It is this pattern I will discuss as it illuminates much about who these children are, how they experience life and the techniques needed to help them in a creative way. For these children, a body-centered approach to play therapy is crucial as is the use or attempted use of the imagination.

Neurologically impaired children lack a psychophysical filter. This filter I am referring to could be described as that invisible but essential device in us that acts like a psychic membrane, protecting us from being flooded by both inner and outer stimuli. Without this filter, children are unable to modulate their aggressive and expressive impulses, nor can they respond to the energy of others without feeling easily overwhelmed. They exist in a state of primary chaos. These children fluctuate between rigidity, as an attempt to filter, and impulsive aggressiveness, either directed at others or in the form of tantrums. This results in a marked defensiveness, often misinterpreted by others and even by themselves. They begin to identify with their defenses, which further distracts from the real issue of their lack of filter. The ideas and play methods described here apply to children with Asperger's and Tourette's Syndrome, neuromuscular disorders, attention deficit disorders and, to a lesser degree, children with learning disabilities.

Sand in itself is a natural filter. It is a material with great malleability and yet potential solidity. It may form the foundation of work with neurologically impaired children as it has this capacity to model filter and mirror it as it develops in the child. I often think that the sand's power is also due in part to its existing in the overlap of sea and earth, possessing the qualities of each. Material that originates from this overlap has the ambivalent looseness needed to provoke the rigidity inherent in most of these children. In combination with the containment of the box and the therapeutic relationship, it becomes a powerful tool. In my experience this filter-building process occurs in the following stages.

## Organized chaos

The inner chaos of the child needs to be expressed. It needs to be part of the therapeutic relationship. It must be accepted, played with, and transformed. The process of expressing this inner chaos through play enables children to recognize it on the instinctual level most available to them. This is especially so with sandplay, in which children are able to actually see and recognize their chaos as such. Robert from Chapter 3 is a perfect example. At the time I was unaware of the neurological implications of his chaotic behavior, but as he expressed his chaos in the sand in our first session and reorganized it, his neurology changed. He has become a prototype for the many children I have seen since with whom I was aware of the neurological issues.

This chaos can be expressed in a variety of ways. It may simply be the sand thrown this way and that, serving as no clear base for anything. Added to this may be a number of figures thrown or carefully placed but in prone positions with no order or focus. The figures are often placed too close to each other to allow them to do anything with each other or relate, or else they may be overlapping or facing every which way. I believe this describes how these children feel and as a result function in social situations.

Sometimes these chaotic scenes begin with a sense of intention or purpose; a knight may be going on a quest, two armies intend to battle, but the chaos that ensues makes everything impossible. We must return to the chaos itself as therein lies the energy for the next step.

With some neurologically impaired children, especially children with Asperger's Syndrome, their first scenes are rigid rather than chaotic. These scenes may depict rows of animals with no purpose (other than perhaps a numerical one) or they may be an exact replication of a story from a movie. There is a sense of purposelessness and lifelessness to them. There is a pointlessness to them that doesn't seem like play. This rigidity eventually gives way to the chaos beneath.

With still other children, this chaos resembles a uroboros, the mythological image of a snake biting its own tail. This uroboric scene may be a long circle of animals, each eating the one in front, or simply moving in a circular pattern. It may be snakes and other reptiles joined in a similar circle of devouring or biting movement. Eventually the circle opens up and everything falls apart. Chaos is ultimately where we begin.

The chaos often goes from seeming static to seeming *charged* and as a result functional over the course of the first several scenes. There is a sense that the chaos has become enlivened, that the pieces are ready to become a whole, and that there is a creative purpose to it. Once this happens, the child's level of functioning in the world begins to improve. This simple truth never fails to astound me. In altering the scene's structure, the child alters their own psycho-physical configuration and to some degree their neurology.

The child is always surprised by the experience of chaos, but recognizes that it is part of them that they want to change. Often this change takes very little time within the context of a creative therapeutic relationship. The structural raw material in the initial chaotic scenes becomes the building blocks for organization.

I would like to describe a few of these opening scene sequences in which chaos becomes functional. A six-year-old girl who was very out of control in school but who had not yet been identified as having a neurological disorder filled the box in her first scene with animals and other figures in random order. She looked puzzled by it but was not ready to change it. She did add several snakes to the scene at the end of her session. She also made a monster drawing of herself that was an attempt at making a cat but it was all jumbled up, looking very much like a tangled ball of thread (Figure 9.1). She said that the monster was "bringing out all of its monster stuff." Her next scene was also just as random but the snakes had jumped up out of the chaos and were sitting along the rim of the box. Her monster this time was more formed with the tangled ball of thread in its stomach (Figure 9.2). She called it "the monster that cried for help." Things were changing inside and out.

In her third scene she made a small hole in the center of the sand and threw several figures in it including the snakes. Then she divided the rest of the box into two sections. In one she placed small building blocks. In the other she placed trees lying down. It was as if containing the chaos in the hole allowed her to consider building something with structural integrity. In

*Figure 9.1 Monster "bringing out all of its monster stuff"*

*Figure 9.2 "The monster that cried for help"*

her next few scenes she spent a long time digging and creating four distinct landforms with water around them. On each of these islands there lived an animal group, such as bears and wildcats. She placed trees on each of these islands. After several sessions she made a land with pathways using the small building blocks. The chaos was gone, as was much of her oppositional behavior in school. She was still a child in need of academic and therapeutic help, but some fundamental changes had been made in her that I believe would make her more social and more educable.

Her original intention to create a scene that was cohesive and her surprise at seeing the chaotic result are typical of opening scenes with neurologically impaired children. Most children with neurological disorders spend their lives unintentionally creating chaos and reacting defensively to it. The world around them reacts to their defensiveness by labeling and medicating without ever truly understanding its source.

This child's placement in the sand and eventual use of materials such as blocks and trees to begin to construct a filter is not unique to her. I have actually tried suggesting that children do so but to no avail. They seem to need to discover it themselves, but making such objects available is a good idea.

As humans we strive to feel integrated above all else. The child with neurological problems is constantly feeling this sense of integrity threatened by their own body and its energy. It is not surprising that they become rigid and inflexible or strike out at the world around them. Their symptoms are often misdiagnosed as oppositional defiant disorder or seen as an anger management issue. When these children are able to organize this chaos and develop a filter, their behavior changes, often quite drastically.

It is really important to have a deeper sandbox than is traditionally used when working with these children. I always use a sandbox that is approximately ten inches deep, although I have several other shallower boxes as well. For children with neurological problems the sand's depth is particularly important, as they need to dig into the material and push the sand around. Their problem involves things being all on the surface in an unprotected and unfiltered state. For them, the path to the symbolic happens in part through a restructuring and digging into the sand itself. With these children in particular, the material becomes an extension of their body and its neurological system. The combination of depth and strong containment is crucial. As therapist and witness, we form part of both the sand's containment and its depth. It is through the relationship we offer that the sand becomes a charged medium and the box a living vessel. They may spend one or many sessions dividing the box into quadrants, filling them in, and then repeating this in variations. Due to the direct relationship between the child's actual neurological system and their handling of the sand, this structural play is pivotal.

## Oppositional play

The second stage of play with these children is oppositional play. This develops quite naturally out of the organized chaos. When the armies are untangled, they can fight. When the building materials and soldiers are standing upright, they can become functional. As the chaos organizes there is usually a gender-based difference in the restructuring of the sand. With boys it is usually a straightforward process in which two clearly defined "sides" are depicted. The sides battle, sometimes endlessly, before the next stage is reached. With girls, the sand is often divided into many islands on which animal life is depicted. There is a sense of defining and diversifying in these scenes. Sometimes girls, and to a lesser extent boys, go through a series of extremely bound scenes in which the central activity has numerous layers of definition: walls of trees, fences, crystal, and shells. I have a fort that children use at this stage to further contain the action. Even this is often not enough and they add layers of other materials as well, such a trees or building blocks. Again, there is a functionalness to this even if it seems excessive.

With boys, this oppositional stage is acted out though battling with me and also through a refusal to lose in any interactions with me. With girls, it takes the form of a dictatorial attitude; I am their assistant in play. They often mercilessly give out orders. The rigidity inherent in their disorders is still present in their newly organized state and will remain so until the next stage is reached.

It is important to tolerate and even encourage this fierce opposition and rule, just as it was important to tolerate their chaos. Eventually, however, I find I must begin to create an insurrection, done in a spirit of playfulness. I introduce new themes or new rules. I confuse the rigidity by switching sides and roles. I begin to play the role of trickster. It is this pushing against them by changing the rules and their pushing back against me in resistance, and also both of us giving in to some extent, that will eventually help the sense of filter to gel.

I also use other materials at this stage, such as clay and building blocks. These materials give children more opportunity to aggress and experiment with form. Both clay and blocks allow for destructive and deconstructive play that often evolves into creative play. What this naturally leads to, slowly but surely, is the next stage.

## Symbolic play

The appearance of symbols in these children's scenes is a hard-won battle and a significant sign of growth. The absence of symbols in the early stages is a result of both the chaos and the unfulfilled need to oppose. It is only when the chaos reorganizes and is solidified and grounded through opposition that the child's body–mind is able to symbolize. Al Lowen in his book *Pleasure* tells us that self-awareness evolves out of self-assertion. Only through asserting ourselves can we come to know ourselves (Lowen 1970). This self-awareness, affirmed through pushing against a person who reacts with a paradoxically firm porosity, is the key to eventual realization and expression with symbols.

In my work with the neurologically impaired child I have come to truly understand the necessity of the use of symbols for normal functioning. They humanize and ground the child, protecting them from the raw intensity of life. They allow for subtlety and secrets. They allow for a deeper and more satisfying articulation of self. They are the filter.

Many years ago I worked with a seven-year-old child whose therapy describes this process of chaos to opposition to symbol really well. Ronald was brought for therapy due to unprovoked aggressive reactions that occurred mainly at home. In school he was overly rigid and well behaved, yet once home he would have numerous aggressive moments. He was always in one of two extremes. The unexplained aggression would then leave him in a defensive and unhappy mood for many hours. He resisted affection and yet seemed to be craving it at the same time. In my first meeting with him, Ronald's physical rigidity was striking. He was eager to play, however, and proceeded to draw a monster. As he was drawing he began to relax and at one point reached over and smacked me on the arm. It didn't hurt but it was a surprise in its seeming to be unconnected to any intentionality. It had just happened. Ronald was quite embarrassed by what he had done, but once I assured him that it was no big deal I asked him if this sort of thing happened often. He assured me that it did, and that when he was in school he kept himself stiff so that he would not do it and get in trouble. No wonder when he came home he needed to discharge.

He went on to make a scene in the sand that started out to be a normal battle scene, with two opposing sides, but it rapidly deteriorated into a mess. Ronald made a valiant effort to keep it organized but just as his body acted impulsively his scene had a life of its own. He was aware of and frustrated by the chaos but managed to enjoy the experience anyway. I think he knew he had an ally in me and sensed the power the sand would come to have for him.

Also, his smacking me was the first time he had ever done so to someone outside of his family. I think this was an important step, probably inspired by his drawing of a monster at my suggestion.

Because he came a very great distance to see me it was decided that he would see me twice in one day, once in the morning and once after lunch. This was Ronald's idea. He told me that in the morning he would play in the sand and in the afternoon we would talk about things, such as how annoying his older brother was. But in fact what this amazing child did was to let his morning sandplay be chaotic and to organize the afternoon scenes. This worked well. He would let all the chaos manifest in his first scene. Sand would fly out of the box, and the story as such would spill over the edge of the box. When he returned after lunch his scene would organize into two rather defined sides battling each other. Initially even in this organized play there was a feeling of underlying chaos but because it had been satiated to some extent in the morning it didn't need to erupt. As a result, this afternoon play quickly became more ordered. He always had me write down the story of the afternoon play.

When he would return after a month or two he would pick up the story from where he had left off as if no time at all had passed. Eventually his morning scenes became an extension of his afternoons, and both were organized and oppositional. The need for two sessions was eliminated and he simply had one longer one. By this time Ronald was a very different child. He had become softer and more affectionate at home with few outbursts and more relaxed at school and more social as a result.

Ronald's first symbol emerged out of his oppositional play in such a subtle way that at first I didn't recognize it as such. In one battle scene a tank appeared that seemed to have many untanklike qualities. This one didn't shoot but rather "it kept things from falling apart." It also built bridges to facilitate freedom of movement. It spoke and it thought. With the emergence of this tank, the battles had begun to take place on different planets and then in parallel universes. This sudden expansion was accompanied by a palpable shift in Ronald's physical and emotional demeanor. He too had expanded. He too was now capable of moving freely from one mode of play to another, from one environment to another.

After my first meeting with Ron I had suggested that his mom have him evaluated for Tourette's. She was open to the idea but it took many months for this evaluation to happen, as she wanted to go to the best pediatric neurologist. When he finally was evaluated he was diagnosed with Tourette's Syndrome but by then his behavior and mood had so greatly improved that there was no need for medication or modification in his school placement. He was now able to modulate and regulate his energy and the tank's appearance was the vehicle and also the expression of this new ability.

The specific first symbols of these children are always very telling. For Ronald the tank expressed solidity and yet it allowed for flexibility. For another boy with Tourette's, his first symbol was a magical substance made out of clay that had "the power to hold things together." The child who made this whispered its name and its power to me and then hid it on a high shelf, checking on it from time to time in subsequent sessions.

The first symbol of a girl with Asperger's was a cave where a treasure was hidden. "I don't know what it is," the girl said to me after creating it, with a mixture of awe and surprise. Prior to this, her play had been very black and white and she had ordered me around like a little Napoleon. She was now becoming able to tolerate the unknown.

These are living symbols and palpable as such when they emerge. Because they have been so absent prior to this, their appearance is a surprise to both the child and myself. The entire space feels numinous and I feel breathless with the awe of the experience.

One boy with neurological and learning issues came initially with great infrequency. His parents just couldn't organize themselves to address his issues with any regularity. I often complained to them that they used therapy "like a band-aid," which became a prophetic comment. Part of the problem was that this boy had a very immediate positive reaction to therapy. He was one of several children with neurological issues who realized early on that if he used two sandboxes, designating one for chaos or as he called it "the mess," then he could let the other be more functional. As a result, he seemed much more functional both in school and at home. I would see him a few times, he would once again organize his chaos and then several months would go by before his parents would call. The school was once again ready to give up and I would see him again. The striking thread through all of this was his lack of symbol formation and as a result his need to continually organize his chaos.

Finally his school and I wisely collaborated and his school required ongoing treatment in order for him to remain there. This did the trick and I saw him regularly. What emerged rather quickly was a symbol, and a very interesting symbol it was. This child, due in part to a night-time seizure disorder, always looked pale faced and drawn, as if he has been vampirized his parents used to say. When he began treatment and stayed the symbol that emerged was blood. He began to grind up red oil crayons and mix them with water and make blood. This he would use to paint with or cover soldiers, often covering himself and me in the process. This blood making elicited several interesting changes in him. He was now often red-cheeked and quite alive looking. Sometimes afterwards he would sing, and one time his mother upon hearing him do so was in tears. "My son doesn't sing!" she assured me. This wave of blood making and bloodletting served some deep emotional and physical purpose for him. It took me a while to recognize it as symbol and not some media-inspired obsession.

The chaos to symbol process may take many months. The organization of the chaos usually occurs rapidly, as seen in the photos. The period of opposition takes the longest and is the most difficult for the therapist (similar to the "terrible twos" for most parents). The birth of symbol happens quite suddenly and always with a sense of surprise. It is usually whispered or spoken in a very different voice and always an obviously numinous moment. With the advent of symbolic play, the child is still neurologically impaired and will resort to rigidity in times of stress, but they are more present and communicative, and thus more human.

I have several extra sandboxes in my office for teaching purposes and these are often used by children to create additional "chapters" – parallel universes or adjoining worlds. These extra boxes can become an important addition for neurologically impaired children. Several children have begun the process of organizing their chaos by making a scene that was totally chaotic in one box and a scene that was organized in the other. It is as if they were winnowing out the chaff from the grain in their lives. Sometimes, symbols appeared very quickly after the chaos was placed in a separate box. The act of discriminating between order and chaos in the use of the two boxes is a natural form of self-assertion that speeds the process of transformation. This will only happen when the child is ready. The use of two boxes can be a brilliant technique, but it must be discovered by the child rather than suggested by the therapist to have the above affect.

I have at times attempted to introduce organization and even symbol when the child was not ready and they willingly obliged me, but the chaos returned. I am always amazed and moved at how easily children will let me know what they need if only I will listen.

Due to the large number of children with neurological disorders I have worked with in the past ten years, I am able to see a consistent pattern that is slowly informing me about their experience of life, both in the obstacles thrown up by their disorders and in the brilliance these disorders afford them. The rapidity with which they express their chaos and begin to organize it into a functional whole and the positive effects this restructuring has on their ability to better negotiate themselves and their world is the most important information to have in working with these children.

Chaos, the dictionary tells us, is "the disorder of formless matter and infinite space, supposed to have existed before the ordered universe"(*Webster's New World Dictionary* 1970). It is this primordial energy of life that the neurologically impaired child must contend with. As it is also from this state that all form arises, these children remain in the place all of us must regress to in order to change deeply. They seem to live closer to "the source."

The number of children developing neurological disorders has risen sharply and will likely continue to do so. Added to this there are many children who have mild neurological features that affect their functioning and their experience of themselves. As these children become an increasing percentage of the population, understanding and treatment from a depth psychology perspective is essential. If we only deal with them through medication or a cognitive-behavioral approach, we miss who they really are. They remain on the surface of themselves, perhaps more functional in the world but having the essence of who they are suppressed. If we let them dive into themselves through the sandplay process, they emerge more intact and integrated. Those with full blown features will always be neurologically impaired and will still need help, patience, and self-understanding. However, the ones with milder neurological features may resolve these completely through the dynamic play therapy process, as it does have the power to profoundly affect body sense, cognitive function, etc.

Children live in or close to an undifferentiated state in which myth is a reality. They flow out into their play and become the objects, the material and the forms. Especially in the context of sandplay it affords them easy access to the wellspring of life.

Chapter 10

# Becoming the Storm
## Using the Energy of Symptoms

I have read that when very large meteors hit the earth they pull up rare and precious metals towards the earth's surface from the power of their impact. The valleys created by these violent collisions become rich sources of ore for ages to come. A similar manifestation occurs when there is a collision between the demands of our external reality and our inner state. When we cannot maintain a functional balance between the two, the resulting symptoms, no matter how disturbing, also contain something invaluable.

Symptoms are the organism's means of alerting the individual, and his or her environment, that something is wrong or out of balance. In that sense, the symptom is a blessing, disturbing as it may be. I have also found that the symptom often contains the very energy, both physical and psychic, needed for growth. This energy has been blocked or thwarted in some way and thus becomes a symptom.

A symptom is like the deeper self crying out. An unacceptable but essential part of the child has been convoluted through repression into something that seems unhealthy but may actually be necessary for the child's well-being. A child may not be able to tolerate feelings of anger or self-assertion, important elements in the child's developing ego, as these feelings are often not approved of by parents or the society in general. The anger and self-assertion turned inwards can reappear as a vast array of symptoms. Some of these symptoms can be quite severe, including suicidal ideation, somatic problems such as encapresis and/or eneurisis, selective mutism, and autistic-like or even psychotic-like behavior. When the feeling and energy trapped in the symptoms become available to the child, the symptoms often go away very quickly and are replaced by vibrancy.

With children the play process can supply the pressure needed to unblock these feelings and energies contained in symptoms or expressed through them. Through sandplay in particular the process of describing one's psycho-energetic state through symbols allows for a change in the inner stasis at the root of most symptoms. In sandplay, this same outpouring of energy and emotion is couched in the language of the imagination. As this process unfolds, symptoms usually disappear. If we to try to annihilate the symptom, we will also annihilate this energy or bury it deeper, only for it to emerge as yet another symptom. Eliminating the symptom that contains some unacceptable but needed aspect of the child means eliminating some of the child's vitality as well. By using the symptom, it transforms into positive life energy available for growth. This transformation often takes place very quickly in children.

The following case illustrates this process well. Six-year-old Michael had developed a phobia of thunderstorms. It had begun at age five as a fear of just thunder and lightning. Soon it had extended to rain and then to clouds in general. His days were consumed with checking the sky for any sign of clouds. At school he began to spend time at the nurse's office and didn't want to attend summer camp for fear it might cloud up while he was there. He was becoming immobilized by his fears.

In my first meeting with him, Michael struck me as a very tense child and afraid of the intensity of his own feelings. His parents were very loving but his mother's rigidity and his father's passivity did not provide an adequate container for his intensity. His parents were not available for him to push against or for him to ground himself through them. This intensity had become split off from him rather than integrated into his personality, and was now becoming "threatening." Often all that is necessary is a simple energetic shift to change profound problems.

Michael's first sand scene was quite flat energetically. A few animals were placed randomly with no relationship to each other and with no central purpose. I have found this to be a typical first scene for the many phobic children I have worked with. A flat, non-dynamic scene is depicted with no real content and parallels the sense of held-in breath and overall stasis often found in these children.

After he made this scene, we talked about his fears. I suggested he become a storm himself and see what would happen. Perhaps if he could become "Hurricane Michael," I suggested, he would feel part of the power of nature and not threatened by it. He understood what I meant on some level and was intrigued by this idea. I began helping him to find ways to do this. At my suggestion, he began to stomp around the room pretending to be a storm while I accompanied him on drums and other percussive instruments. His storm picked up intensity as the tempo of the music increased. I tried to duplicate his energy with the instruments but also subtly expand it to allow his storm to become bigger and louder.

He explored various other means of "storming," throwing pillows and leaping onto them and flinging them into the air and seemed quite happy in the process. He then went back to the sandbox and added two wolves to his scene. These wolves were howling and "waking up the other animals."

Michael's second scene continued from where he had left it the week before. He placed wolves in the sand first this time and other animals in groups of three of four. They were beginning to form families and clans. This was an important step. Michael spent a great deal of time exploring the idea of storms and storming. He put on a puppet show about a wizard who made storms come and go. The wizard, directed by a prince, was using the storm to scare his father and mother. At times the wizard would literally be "caught up" in his own storms. This puppet show was a collaboration between Michael and myself. I would lead at times and he at others. He needed my confidence in his ability to embody and negotiate his aliveness. It was awkward in the way that attempting to change and grow always is. Neither of us knew from moment to moment what might happen, and whether the phobia was indeed transforming itself as we danced and played. Michael then did more storm dances with my musical accompaniment. The volume and intensity of these storms was increasing. He seemed to physically grow larger as he danced his storm dance

His third scene the following week included a wizard figure (similar to the figure in his puppet show) that lived in a cave with a candelabrum where he practiced his magic. The next week the wizard had two candelabra and two other forms of fire in his cave. His cave or fortress was literally filled with fire. The feeling around this fire in the mountain was one of power but also containment. I was reminded of a hexagram in the I Ching that is an archetype for growth. The various configurations placed around the cave became more complicated and articulate. Michael was now collecting the power and aliveness, symbolized by the fire, that he had become disconnected from and viewed as threatening.

Michael was now much less afraid of the weather in his daily life. He "got a little nervous" when it rained at camp one day, but otherwise was becoming able to handle the external storms in his life. He was also becoming more outspoken at home and asserting himself with both parents more frequently.

Michael's sandplay quickly became more diversified and complex. The storyline developed from one-dimensional to multidimensional. As he became more capable of experiencing and regulating his own intensity, his scenes became more complicated and intelligent, but also focused.

His final sand scenes were entitled "family reunions" and involved extremely complicated interactions that all related to the central theme of a joyous and much anticipated reunion. These reunions were clearly about an inner reintegration. They included buried treasures, dragons hovering, and groups of knights jousting. There were also groups of boys going on adventures and playing tricks on each other, as well as a fortress in the center filled with houses, parties and fire pits. There was a feeling of abundant life in these scenes.

Michael was now free of his phobia. He was more outgoing and expressive than his parents. They were attentive parents, but fearful and apprehensive in their relationship to the world. Perhaps Michael unconsciously sensed this about his parents and his symptoms were expressing the thwarted energy in the family as well as in himself. Through Michael's growth, his parents also changed and grew. The family reunion theme in Michael's scenes was literal as well as symbolic.

The various symbols and symbolic themes in Michael's scenes were also a part of the healing process. He placed wolves in his scene after he became more aggressive. He placed fire in his scenes after his own inner fire of life became more acceptable to him. The use of these symbols reinforced the development of these qualities in him. The mixture of sound and fire is basic to the idea of storms, but also basic to the growth of a child. The child needs to make noise to have his or her needs met and also to discharge the tensions of daily life. The child's fiery passion and life force must be tolerated and even encouraged. The alternative can lead to a disconnection of this energy in the child and begin to feel threatening rather than enlivening as a result.

Many of the children in these pages used the energy of their symptoms. The chaos-filled children with neurological disorders used their chaos to organize. Children who were fallen apart used this metaphorically to reassemble in a more functional form. The ashen-faced child who endlessly made blood in some mysterious way used his symptom. The child who couldn't stand on his own two feet and then slipped on ice used his symptom. Using a symptom playfully and creatively is using what the child is bringing with them as raw material for change. No leap is needed to engage them, as the energy needed to change is embedded in the symptom itself. The leap may come when the symptom dissolves and the child accesses the underlying energy. Michael literally danced his way to health.

When symptoms are only seen as negative rather than as a possibility for growth, they can become deep-seated problems. They can be the very impetus for transformation. If the fears and symptoms in children are creatively engaged in the context of play, they can become doorways. Connecting with the child's vitality and wildness, personified so perfectly in the thunderstorm, becomes a key capable of unlocking almost any door.

Chapter 11

# Finding the Treasure

One of the most common events that occurs in the sandbox in sandplay therapy is the hiding and finding of buried treasure. Many children, especially young ones, can do it endlessly. It is very frustrating to new therapists who are longing for scenes with symbols to interpret, not this endless burying and unearthing. Yet this act is itself a symbol, as well as a use of the substance of the sand, its multidimensionality, its depth. Usually all this unearthing leads somewhere. After a period of hiding and finding things, another level of play develops that has a sense of the sand's depth but tells a story, expressing a more complex tale.

A five-year-old boy was recently referred to me for social problems. His teacher felt he had no individual identity. He never used the word "I" and was unable to relate to his peers as a result. His speech was indistinct also, but a speech and language evaluation found no actual speech problem. In my first few sessions with him he spent all of the time digging in the several boxes I have in my office, ignoring the many figures that line my walls and in many ways ignoring me, or using me as an assistant in his digging. He found many crystals and shiny marbles left in the sand by other children as he dug and was thrilled by this. His mother was amazed at his willingness to come see me, and the ease of his separation from her. She reported that he was very happy after our first few visits, yet he had done nothing but dig.

I began to introduce figures into his digging that seemed related to what he was doing. Dragons came to compete with him for the treasures he was finding. Although he rejected them at first I could see that he was also intrigued by them. He quickly came to incorporate them into his play as if he had "discovered" them, just as he had the gems in the sand.

Slowly but surely he began to create stories, expand his repertoire and relate to me as me. His imagination was very rich and his stories once they came were quite advanced for his age. The sense of "I" that his teacher had noticed an absence of emerged with great strength when it finally did. I would say he was more self-possessed than most children I have worked with once he arrived. Likewise, I found him to be more relational than many children once he began to do so. His vocabulary as his speech became clear was very advanced. It was as if this gem of a child was himself hidden, waiting to be found. He used the sand as a grounding medium to help give external form to this buried internal sense of "I."

My tolerating his endless treasure hunting while I paradoxically tempted him by adding new variables was a key to unlocking the problem. Children will do anything to maintain their sense of integrity. They may become oppositional, regress, become passive and withdrawn or even become physically ill. The golden treasure of self may be hidden so deeply within the child that we can no longer see any sign of it. Yet even the most damaged child retains this self, at least potentially.

Our job as therapists in light of this becomes nothing short of a quest, in the mythical sense. We must align ourselves with the child by first honoring their defenses, by first speaking their language in order to begin the quest. This alignment is done not as a manipulation but out of deep respect for the child, even the defenses they had erected which they must ultimately shed. As in so many folk tales and quest stories, when we show this respect we are given clues and maps that will help us to proceed. The path to be followed reveals itself through the child's fantasies, play configurations and spontaneous movements.

The above child unburied himself and went on into life with ease, a healthy, loved child who had somehow simply gotten stuck. Not all children emerge with such grace. Not all children have been loved and protected enough that descent into the sand with the right guide and guardian can so easily unearth the treasure. Many children's treasure is buried deep and the discovery of it is hard earned and the path to it an erratic one. The following case is an example.

Peter began working with me when he was five years old. His parents had described Peter as seeming normal until approximately two and a half years of age. At this point he reportedly regressed overnight into a withdrawn, non-speaking child who was in his own world. During this period in his life his parents fought frequently, often quite violently. His father was extremely angry and prone to violent acts, though not towards his son. His mother was a depressed, "ghost-like" woman. Both must have been terrifying to a young child. Neither acted like caregivers, although they wanted to be. Peter's parents separated and he and his older brother lived with their father, as their mother was incapable of caring for them. There was more stability in this household, but no mother figure. When I began seeing Peter he saw his mother infrequently. He spent his days in day care where the teacher had repeatedly urged both parents to seek help for Peter, who was really quite autistic-like in all respects.

At the onset of treatment, Peter's speech was inarticulate. Even his brother, with whom he was quite close, could rarely understand him. His brother believed that most of the time Peter was telling stories based on television shows and movies he had seen. Peter's body was rigid and yet his arms were limp and his hands cold to the touch. His facial expression was one of surprise, with a slight lift to the eyebrows. He was attached to his parents but expressed this in a shadow-like manner, following along after them but not interacting with them.

Prior to meeting Peter I encouraged his parents to find a school placement for him that would be therapeutic without necessarily being a special education setting. They did so and approximately one and a half months after I began working with Peter he started school in what turned out to be a very good placement. I also urged his mother and father to reconcile their differences enough so that Peter might see his mother more frequently, who through her own therapy was in a better position to mother him. This also began to take place.

Peter entered the play space without any reluctance, and without any affect at all. Once we were alone face to face, it was obvious that my only means of really interacting with him would be through mirroring, that is, using his body language as a means of trying to speak to him. In response to my introducing myself, he uttered several unintelligible phrases and pointed to his chest. I followed suit, uttering my own version of those phrases or sounds and pointing to my chest. Peter responded immediately by exaggerating his movements and sounds, adding a bucking-like motion to his movement phase. We began a dance/dialogue in which I repeated his various expressions, trying to feel what it felt like within my own body to do these, hoping to begin to enter his world. At one point Peter began to laugh. I think he was both amazed and tickled at my efforts to reach him. No one had ever spoken with him on this level. His movements continued to have two aspects: pounding or poking at his chest as he thrust it out and leaping upwards. It was as if he was trying to spark life into his body. Peter was either active like this or totally still, with limp arms and a vacant facial expression. These moments of blankness had a seizure-like quality but neurological testing revealed no abnormalities. Where was he then when he went away like that?

After several sessions, comprised of this pattern, I grew impatient to find a means of moving with Peter that could evolve more. I suggested we take off our shoes and sit on the ground facing each other. As Peter was very compliant he did so. Our feet were approximately one foot apart. I waved my feet and toes around, both initiating movements and repeating movements that Peter's feet had made.

We did a little foot dance and Peter seemed quite delighted with it. His feet began to "run away," hiding behind him and then peeking out at me. I responded with a combination of mirroring, provocation and simply staying still. Peter let me know what he wanted from me as a response, communicating this non-verbally.

Over the next several visits these foot dialogues or dramas continued to evolve. Sometimes Peter's feet would stomp or kick. I would encourage this by putting a pillow under his feet so it wouldn't hurt. At other times his feet would attack my feet, always quite playfully. Peter's speech became clearer and I could begin to understand the stories he was relating to me. They were all about Superman or Superboy. It turns out that he had been trying to tell me, by poking at his chest, that Superman's power came from there, that it would fly out or leap up in him. Superboy was closer to his heart, obviously who he would have liked to be. These surges of energy that leapt up in him seemed to need grounding, as they kept him disconnected. The foot games were in fact serving as a grounding exercise without me quite realizing it.

Peter's foot dialogues evolved to a standing position, so that when his feet ran away all of him would leave, going to a far corner of the room behind a chair. Still his feet led the way, hiding for varying lengths of time, and these periods of "charged" stillness were notable in their contrast to the vacant stillness of his former sessions. At one point his feet stayed away a very long time. I could sense that he was waiting, and insisting that I wait too. After what seemed like ages, he peeked around the edge of the chair.

What was critical, and I do mean critical, was that I allowed Peter to be in charge of the timing. For when he emerged around the corner of the chair, it was truly he. Some basic sense of self was now looking out at me. Like the little girl who peaked out the window in Chapter 3, this was really *he*. He had begun to emerge from his shell.

In Peter's next session he entered a new phase of play, which spanned several weeks. It was still about emerging, but quite different. The child who had been in my office prior to Peter had created a "hideout" with a blanket and two chairs. Peter indicated that he wanted to fly to another planet, using the "hideout" as our spaceship. Peter's speech by now was more developed.

Though still unable to say "I want," he was able to make his wants known. He instructed me to be the pilot of our spaceship. At a signal from him we landed on another planet. Peter stepped out and went to my bookshelf and spent time touching everything on the shelf, naming each object out loud to me as if he was naming new discoveries and as the discoverer was entitled to pick a name for each. Despite the humor in this fantasy, it was obviously a very important step.

Then he returned to the ship and we went to another planet. Here again Peter went to another place in my office, this time a shelf with stones and shells on it, and again spent time discovering and naming each item before returning to the ship. He then indicated that we should return to Earth; enough discovering for the time being.

This phase of Peter's therapy, which spanned several visits, was truly about orienting, in which he established himself in time and space. He was re-entering the world he had fled from at age two and a half and did so in a way that kept his integrity intact. By pretending to be the first one to discover the world and its objects, it became *his* world, not the world of his parents that he had originally rejected.

Peter went on to make use of the objects he had discovered in subsequent sessions. He had "discovered" my sandbox and the miniatures which children use in it. He began to play with these, first by simply setting them up on the edge of the sandbox and knocking them down, laughing uproariously each time. He then went on to use the figures as actual figures, not simply objects of his vengeful aggression.

He went through a phase of making buildings for army men to hide in. These buildings were often destroyed and rebuilt again and again. Eventually Peter came to use the sandbox itself, and to create scenes in it.

Peter's first actual scene portrayed two men pouring water that became a river flowing down a mountain. At the bottom of the mountain was a cave that the river flowed into. Peter told me that "the treasure" was in that cave and that the two men were helping it to grow. Here Peter was describing what he and I had been doing all along and towards what end. That he was able to express this in symbolic form was extremely significant, and also very satisfying. The capacity to symbolize requires a certain level of growth and earmarks it. It signifies humanization. And Peter now seemed truly more human. The wooden, almost zombie-like quality that had at first dominated his demeanor had slowly melted. He now seemed like a child, soft and vulnerable but also vibrant.

Peter drew three monster drawings for me during the course of his treatment. The first was done in our second or third meeting, and it was a tangle of lines and shapes with no concrete from. The second drawing was done during the aggressive phase in which Peter experimented with knocking things down. Peter named this second monster "Makahak" and with great pleasure told me that Makahak "rises up out of the ground and punches people in the balls."

Peter's third drawing was done on one of his final visits with me. The body itself had gelled; it now had definition and boundaries. Peter dubbed him "Grass Grinder" and informed me, "He grinds a bunch of grass and runs through the rain to find some soil to plant it in." With the monster's defini-tion and boundaries comes the power to run and also to keep things secret. The monster is holding the grass behind his back.

Peter now felt secure enough to move into a symbolic realm of speaking in which things could be planted, with the assuredness that they would grow. The rain and the soil and Peter's whole demeanor at this point reflected fertility. The combination of power, mystery and even poetry in this drawing had the earmarks of self.

In what became Peter's final scene with me, the cave with the treasure in it was again depicted, this time with a two-headed dragon standing guard. Peter let me have a very brief peak at the treasure that he had placed inside. This was his way of thanking me for helping him to find it, and I could think of no better form of thanks.

Peter's progress in school and in life was quite steady once he had emerged from his shell via our movement interchange. He would "space out" periodically, at which times he would resemble his old self. This usually occurred when he was angry. His teacher was very helpful in those moments, confronting him with his feelings and bringing the anger out, even allowing herself to be the focus of it.

Slowly but surely Peter became more social, made academic strides and in general normalized. He eventually entered a regular school setting and was adjusting fairly well. I don't know if this growth continued without support after I stopped seeing him. His last monster "Grass Grinder" was a huge leap for him both cognitively and emotionally, but it was still quite primitive. As I look back at Peter from the wisdom of time and distance there were neurological features to his play and his body sense, despite a neurologist saying he was fine. Perhaps he needed the intervention of an occupational therapist. Perhaps his involvement in martial arts would do the trick. But he "arrived on the planet" so to speak in his work with me, emerging out of chaos into a very solid and perhaps too solid form.

All children contain the treasure that Peter let me help him to nourish and eventually let me catch a glimpse of. This treasure is often buried deep and out of reach. Perhaps all of life's striving is to be able to locate this inner treasure. All children need to feel this treasure, its worth and its power, in order to feel whole. And I do not believe that many children do feel it – not simply the children I work with who have obvious problems or parents who recognize this lack, but most children. I have many objects in my miniature collection that children designate as treasures, such as crystals, golden goblets, magic lamps, treasure chests, etc. They get used repeatedly, buried and unearthed again and again. But the real treasure must emerge from within the child, just as the images that have real healing power are created out of the child and not selected off a shelf. It will only be revealed, if it is to be revealed, after much work.

The little boy who dug for many sessions eventually found himself as a result. By traveling to distant planets and claiming them as his discovery Peter was also affirming his own aliveness, also discovering himself.

Chapter 12

# Closing Scenes

The closing scenes with which children terminate therapy should ideally indicate a resolution of the conflicts that their opening scenes at the onset of therapy expressed. As in the case of many dramas, it is not so much an end as a beginning. The resolution of a conflict always brings with it this sense of new possibilities, of the potential to live life in a new and healthier way. A sense of closure and, as a result, peace will be apparent in many of these closing scenes.

Because growth and change will hopefully be an ongoing process for each child we see, we may often not get a clear sense of the end, but rather that a place has been reached from which more growth can occur in its own time. The story is a work in progress in other words. But there are children who will give us a sense of the story being completed, and it is often those whose life situation is in need of a true transformation.

Seven-year-old Emily, whose monster named "Mouth" opened Chapter 1, had been referred for therapy by her school as a result of habitual masturbation. The effect of this self-stimulation was to render her "out of it," which was preventing her from learning.

On Emily's first visit, after drawing herself as a huge monster with blood dripping fangs, she created the following scene:

> On a hill, a fortress lay half in ruins. Inside it a pillar of gold stood. Down below in a valley a battle was being waged by a group of knights. Emily described her scene as follows: "Someone has attacked the fortress and is trying to steal the gold. The knights are trying to protect it."

The scene describes a split in Emily – her inner state, the threatened treasure, and her outer state in which her defenses are struggling to protect this inner treasure, this sense of integrity and of self. Emily's monster hinted at buried rage and her scene described, albeit in symbolic language, the cause of this rage: that is, she felt under attack.

Emily's father expected perfection from her and from himself as well. He was rigid, compulsive and very vocal when his high expectations were not lived up to. The tension that this created in the household was constant, which further fueled her father's angry outbursts. Emily's mother sided with her daughter but was too intimidated by her husband to stop him. With education and support from me, Emily's father was able to make significant changes in how he dealt with Emily. Often parents know they are making major mistakes and want desperately to change but can't seem to step out of their negative behavior patterns on their own. It takes an outside force, as well as education about how to foster healthy children, to bring about change.

Emily's second scene described a deeper level of her problem. Horses were penned up in the center of the box. From the hills around the horses came panthers, descending to kill them. One panther was placed atop a horse, in the act of tearing its flesh.

Emily's scene and her description of it contained much tension and emotion. It was a very painful scene to witness, depicting as it did so graphically how her own innate power, represented by the panthers, had been turned on herself, on her deeper instinctual self, represented by the horses. In light of this, her self-stimulating behavior can be seen as Emily striking inward at herself instead of outward at her father and mother. Clawing at herself, like the panther on the horse, she was left in a stupor, unable to think or relate.

After creating her second scene, Emily went on to talk about a girl she knew "who made her so angry she wanted to burn her house down." She also spoke about her cat "that was so brave it would chase dogs out of the yard." She shared this while smashing a large piece of clay. Here was a first movement outward of her anger and aggression, reflected in both her comments and her body movements.

Both the wildcat and the horse are totemic symbols used repeatedly by girls in their play therapy. The cat is a symbol of feminine power. Emily mentioned it twice in her second session in two very different contexts. The horse, on the other hand, is a symbol for girls of the instincts and the instinctual part of the self, thus the great appeal to many girls of horses and horseback riding. I have not yet worked with a girl who has not used the horse symbol at some time in their therapy process. In Federico Fellini's film *Juliet of the Spirits*, made I am told while Fellini was in therapy with Jung or at least a Jungian, the horse is a central symbol in Juliet's transformation process. Juliet's first vision in the film is of a raft of dead horses, a sign that her instinctual self is as if dead. Emily's horses weren't dead but on their way to being so.

During subsequent sessions Emily continued to create scenes in which horses were being attacked by wildcats. She continued to describe these in graphic terms, but the mood was beginning to shift. These descriptions had lost some of their horror. Meanwhile she evolved her creation of monsters from two-dimensional drawings to three-dimensional clay monsters. The multidimensionality of clay is for many children a much more satisfying means of expressing and especially exploring their aggression. It also lends itself to a fluid evolution of form. A huge monstrous thing can become something beautiful or mysterious with ease, as in the case of Sarah from Chapter 2, whose monster became a fountain. This facile quality makes it a very important tool, used second only to the sand in my office. It is a very good means for children beginning to embody aggression.

Emily really took to the clay. At first the monsters she made were simply statues, but eventually they came to life. On one visit she had me make a clay monster as well and our monsters battled each other. She became very bold in her attacks, taking great pleasure in smashing my monsters. I have used this technique with thousands of other children since with great results. She devised ways of tricking my monster into remaining unguarded and then would pounce on it. She got louder each time she destroyed me.

One day Emily came in and created the same castle scene as in her first visit. This time, however, the castle walls were very solid. They had been reconstructed, so to speak. Looking at Emily as she created this I realized that she too had become more solid. In school her self-stimulating behavior had disappeared and she was engaging in some verbal battles with her class-mates.

The following session was Emily's last. She entered the play setting and swaggered over to the sandbox. From the timid child I met several months earlier she had become capable of swaggering! She grabbed a wooden pillar from the box of blocks and slammed it down into the center of the sand. "There!" she proclaimed in a *very* loud voice. Then she began to cover the pillar with sand, creating a mountain. The mountain had a waterfall running down it and was encircled by a river. She then placed horses all over the mountain and christened it "Horse Mountain." She then added a small bridge from the mountain over the river "so the horses could leave when they wanted."

The scene was a wonderful statement of strength, with a balance of feminine and masculine qualities. Emily was very satisfied with it as she stood back to survey it, and seemed very satisfied with herself as well. She then ran to a group of puppets in my office and began to act out the following play: A princess lived with her mother and father, the king and queen. She also had a pet dragon, unbeknownst to them, which she kept in the garden. The princess would lure her parents out into the garden and the dragon would gobble them up, belching loudly afterwards.

Emily repeated this play several times with great delight, getting louder and louder each time. It was almost inconceivable that such a small child could produce the volume of sound which she did that day. Eventually Emily's catharsis subsided. She left very happy and conveyed to her parents a lack of enthusiasm about coming again. This didn't surprise me.

Emily's final scene ended with a bang. Many children's therapy ends on a quieter note. The themes of previous sessions will often be woven together in a manner that expresses completeness. Or, in other cases, the child may play quietly, all the tension and emotion gone from their play configurations. In these moments they may even ask "Why do I come here?" or even "What do you do for a living?" – ironically, recognizing for the first time that there might be something unusual about our relationship. In these cases the question is really a statement: "I don't need to come any more."

For many children the experience of growth and change that therapy offers is merely a first step. Whether they resume therapy later on or simply continue to grow via life experiences, they may pick up the thread again. Some children's sessions end with a sense of this loose thread waiting to be picked up again.

William was a child, alluded to briefly in Chapter 3, who always created two worlds in his sand scenes, an outer and an inner world. The outer world, created on the surface of the sand, was rather boring and lifeless, but the one alluded to beneath the surface of the sand, sometimes indicated by a doorway, was vast and beautiful. It was here that William's true self resided.

His family was moving away and in his last visit with me he finally allowed the lower and inner world to erupt, destroying the upper world or actually mixing the two worlds together. He had created a new material out of this mix as a result with which he could deal with life more effectively. This new material would need to be experimented with. This probably would take the form of standing up for himself in school with peers and with his parents. He might return again to therapy briefly at some integral points in his life. Yet his last session reflected the intermingled substance of self about to be worked with – an end to the old way of being and a new beginning.

It is always best to end treatment when the child asks to. It's hard for most parents to believe that such a day will ever come. Usually at the onset of therapy their children are so eager to come that parents fear it will become a habit, a dependency. Yet I have never worked with a child who did not lose interest in coming once it was not meeting a therapeutic need. Once the conflict is resolved the child will want to use the energy and strength regained to go forwards into life. Their peers are always better playmates than I am. I do not play board games or card games with children. The play is always creative and geared towards the disorganizing–reorganizing process that is therapy. Thus it is only appealing when this is the need. When the play I engage them in (or vice versa) is no longer content full, no longer charged, the child loses interest in it.

Again, I am not trying to simply eliminate symptoms but to help the child become healthy. Jung used the word individuation to designate the process of personality development that leads to the fullest possible actualization of the self. Individuation means becoming a single, homogenous being, and insofar as individuality embraces our innermost, last and incomparable uniqueness it also implies becoming one's own self. We could, therefore, translate individuation as coming to self-hood or self-realization (Jung 1961).

Whatever therapeutic work we do must be towards this end. Otherwise however many symptoms we have helped eliminate, sublimate or redirect, we have not done much really.

Five-year-old Jacob began treatment in the midst of his parents' long and ugly divorce, with sleep disturbances, repeated illnesses and general fearfulness. His pediatrician recommended play therapy as a means of addressing his frequent sickness as well as the other symptoms. When he began therapy he seemed like a serious, stiff and unhappy adult. He was cautious of anything "playful" although somewhat intrigued also. He preferred to draw pictures that, although imaginative, were more concerned with accuracy than pleasure. Over time as he experimented with play and aggressiveness he also began to loosen up. Through fighting with me and using the tennis racket on a mattress, he became less afraid of the intensity of his own and his parents' emotions.

In one particular session he began to talk about how angry his parents were at each other. "My dad's afraid of my mom," he realized. With only a little help from me he added, "And my mom's afraid of my dad." At this point he laughed for quite a while, saying he was laughing because the whole thing was so silly, but also laughing with relief. He had reduced his parents' conflicts to the childish level from which they really arose. This ironically made them more understandable and less terrifying.

Jacob loved to draw and his drawings were unusually advanced technically for his age. He was very concerned that they should be so, that people might see them and admire them for seeming to be done by a much older child. After Jacob began to loosen up in his play and in his concerns about his parents, he drew a monster that was quite unusual for him. It was very sloppily drawn and looked very wild (Figure 12.1). The monster's name was "Ugu Ugu" and he began to talk to me. His speech was a mixture of gibberish and babytalk. Jacob laughed with pure delight at his creation, the first laugh I had ever heard from him. In Jacob's next visit he drew another monster, a further evolution of Ugu Ugu. This ones name was "Ugu Ga Ga Huhu Gee Gee Gu Gee Goo Goo" (Figure 12.2).

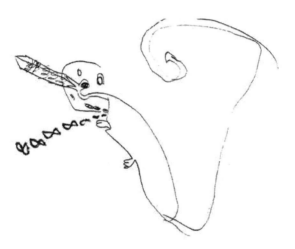

*Figure 12.1 Monster talking babytalk: "Ugu Ugu"*

Jacob's monsters were regressing but in the service of his ego. Whereas many children regress when confronted with ego-threatening circumstances, Jacob had begun acting instead like a little adult. His symptoms, however, belied this external maturity. As he progressed in his therapy, he regressed to strengthen his ego. Over the following weeks his babytalking monsters became both wilder and more amorphous. They seemed to be disintegrating. And as they fell apart Jacob's false self did also. He became happier and much more confident.

*Figure 12.2 Further evolution of "Ugu Ugu"*

His monsters then began to re-form into dragons. He created one spectacular dragon-monster that was in part inspired by a statue of the Hindu god Shiva that I have in my office (Figure 12.3). Here was a splendid combination of form and wildness. It expressed balance. Shiva is the Hindu god of destruction and rebirth, and of reproduction, a fitting theme for what was one of Jacob's last visits.

*Figure 12.3 Dragon-monster in pose of the Hindu god Shiva*

Jacob took a break for a few weeks but then requested to come back. In this visit he created a sand scene in which a dragon was battling with a powerful knight. The dragon was slain and Jacob gave a long and *very* loud vocal description of the dragon's death. The dragon sank down into the sand as it died. Then with an upsurge of energy the dragon emerged, reborn. This death and rebirth scenario was repeated several times with great volume and vibrancy.

Finally the dragon remained alive, a balance of power having been achieved. The knight and the dragon were now one energetic entity. The absolute delight on his face and the enormous volume he was now capable of were so striking in contrast to the sullen repressed child I had met initially. It was possible Jacob might want to come again at some point to continue to solidify his newfound strength.

Chapter 13

# The Dragon

In the previous chapter Jacob made use of the most powerful and important of all symbols which appear in children's therapy – that of the dragon. The dragon is the ultimate symbol of aliveness, and yet it is more than this. When it manifests itself in a child's scenes, stories or play configurations it is almost always a sign that some profound change is taking place. In my puppet collection, the dragon puppet is by far the most frequently used, the central character in numerous spontaneous puppet shows. More importantly, it is the puppet which children select as their emissary, the one that they most want to be.

Because of its central significance to the child's healing process, it merits looking at the dragon symbol more closely. The great eighteenth-century artist, poet, and mystic William Blake introduces two different dragon figures in his writings that feel similar to the child's use of the symbol in therapy. In his *The Marriage of Heaven and Hell* we encounter the dragon-man. June Singer, in her classic work on Blake, *The Unholy Bible*, describes this dragon-man as "the arbiter between the feminine and masculine principles. He serves the transcendent function of mediating between the two and making a new development possible" (Singer 1986, p.132).

The other dragon-like figure we encounter in Blake's works is that of Orc. Orc is the name Blake gives to the personification of Revolution in the material world. Blake lived in a period of revolution, the American and French Revolutions being two examples. Orc is this revolutionary energy that must be brought into play in order for major changes to occur.

These two qualities, that of revolution and that of mediating between the masculine and feminine function towards wholeness, are keys to understanding and appreciating the dragon symbol as children use it. In working with the troubled child we seek to foster a revolution, not only in their own psyche but also it is hoped within the family system they are part of as well. Yet we are also eager for the child to achieve a sense of inner balance. The child's aliveness needs constraints. Within the right framework the child may actually produce or ask for these constraints themselves, as we have seen in the numerous cases cited thus far.

Boys use the dragon symbol in a very different context in their therapy process than girls, and this difference is a fascinating one. With both the dragon is often an amoral but never an immoral character. With both, the dragon's destructiveness has a positive purpose. The dragon is never portrayed as the enemy. He is always aligned with life, but life at its deepest and highest potential. When the dragon destroys life it does so to preserve life, which is ideally the spirit in which revolution occurs. The American Revolution is an example of this.

With boys the dragon must be fought with initially. It may be conquered, but if so will be resurrected, often rising out of its own ashes like the mythical phoenix. The dragon may destroy others but only to protect itself or the "treasures" which it often guards. This "treasure" is rarely monetary, but has to do with power. It may be a well with magical powers, a cave full of crystals that have power, or a child who may one day be a powerful hero.

One boy created a memorable sand scene in which almost all of the figures in my miniature collection were charging up a large, wave-like mountain. At the crest of this wave/mountain stood a dragon. The boy finished his scene just as his father arrived to pick him up. The father, on seeing the sand scene, remarked that it looked like the evil dragon would surely be slain by the hordes charging up the mountain. His son looked at him in disbelief. "Are you crazy?" he exclaimed. "The dragon is the good guy. They just don't understand him. But they can't destroy him, so don't worry!" His father seemed more worried at the idea of an indestructible dragon. This boy had been brought for therapy due to overly aggressive behavior in school. Ironically, this dragon began appearing as a symbol in his scenes at the same time as he became able to exercise self-control over his impulses.

In the case of girls, the dragon symbol appears in a very different context. It always *belongs* to the heroine of the scene or story. Frequently it is described as "the princess's" pet. Often this pet is unknown to others, as in the case of the princess whose pet dragon lived in a castle garden, unbeknownst to the king and queen. Translating this common theme we could say the girl feels a connectedness and even a sense of ownership with the power of life. But this truly wonderful attribute goes unseen and unappreciated by the world around her (and eventually by the child herself).

Girls who manifest this symbol in their therapy are real dynamos underneath but have been forced to repress this strength, usually turning it on themselves in the process. The dragon often appears at a point in therapy when the child has ceased to do so. Initially it appears for the purpose of avenging the girl. This revenge is in the service of healing the child's wounded sense of self. The following case explores the importance of the dragon symbol for the girl in more detail.

Meg was brought for therapy at the age of ten in the wake of her parents' divorce. She came with a long list of symptoms, including physical complaints such as stomach aches and headaches, no friends, self-deprecating and suicidal comments, to name only a few. Meg's mother described her daughter as very quiet and "laid back like her father," who was unwilling to meet with me because he "didn't believe in therapy." Meg's mother, in contrast, was very emotional, loud and a bit frenetic. She had been "too much" for her ex-husband. Both parents were very strict with Meg.

Meg struck me at our first meeting as an exceptionally bright and gifted child. Although she made almost no eye contact, she was very eager to talk and expressed herself very well. She was not shy or "laid back" but rather repressed and thwarted. She was delighted that I had a sandbox and eagerly made the following elaborate scene.

> In a corner of the scene on a high mountain, a princess stood with a dragon. Meg informed me as she placed it there that I needn't worry, that the dragon belonged to the princess. Down below in a valley several situations were being played out, all with a common theme. In one spot a female dancer was being thrown into a volcano by a tribe of people, "as a sacrifice." In another spot a group of witches were about to kill a young girl, again, "as a sacrifice."
>
> In another spot the girl's mother, the queen, was searching for her lost daughter. She had to pass through a forest in which a snake would definitely turn her to stone. The last item Meg placed was a knight who was struggling to reach the princess and save her from the dragon. Meg commented that the knight was wasting his energy, that the princess was happy with her dragon.

The central theme of Meg's scene was of females being sacrificed. Meg was speaking about her own inner state. Meanwhile an element of her true self, the princess and the dragon part, remained intact but separate.

It took very little support on my part for Meg's natural aggressiveness and expressiveness to redirect itself. She spent time in her first visit pounding on the mattress in my office, venting her frustration at her parents and her peers. I'm sure that an adult male encouraging this helped facilitate the rapid changes that occurred in Meg. By the time I saw her a second time, her mother was reporting a much happier and also a more outspoken child at home. Meg's mother, with a lot of support from me, was able not only to tolerate this but to actually encourage it. She realized that she had been similar as a child. Her authoritarian father had beaten her into submission and her energy and enthusiasm had become a chronic hyperactiveness instead. She didn't want this for her child.

Meg's third visit produced the following sand scene. A witch was about to be burned at the stake. The witch's mother and daughter, both witches as well, called for help from "the forces of nature." Just as the burning was about to take place, a dragon came from over the mountains and wildcats leapt up from out of the ground. The villagers either ran off in fear or were killed. The witch was saved and could now "live in peace."

Meg's personal life began to blossom. When we first met she had felt very victimized by her peers, often the brunt of much teasing. This had changed and some of the people she had feared most were now becoming her friends. She had also scored so well on a scholastic test that she had been chosen to participate in a very prestigious summer program at a famous university.

The one area of life still blocked was her relationship with her father. He was extremely rigid and expected Meg to be obedient at all times. She still feared him, remembering spankings administered for the least amount of opposition on her part. We discussed ways in which she might begin to assert herself with him.

Meg's next sand scene, after several visits, was quite different. It portrayed a land where males were not allowed and where females lived in happiness and peace. It was a lovely, magical place in which each female had her own living space, coexisting harmoniously with each other and with nature. Many of the women and girls lived in seashells. The central figure was a princess who lived with her pet dragon in a large shell. If a man entered this domain he was escorted to a patch of quicksand and disposed of.

Meg's first two scenes had not only a dragon in them but witches as well. Historically, witch was a term used to label and condemn women, in particular women who acted autonomously. In the first scene, the witches are killing a young girl, whose mother will not be able to save her. In the second scene the witches are now aligned with the mother and the daughter and unified in their efforts. That they survive, with the help of a dragon, is not only a relief but also a sign that an important shift has taken place in Meg. By the third scene, the witches are gone and we have simply womankind, coexisting, safe, strong, and happy.

Meg was proclaiming her autonomy. She was immensely satisfied with her scene. Afterwards she allowed me to speak with her mother about the situation between Meg and her father. She promised to speak with him about it, and although doing so elicited a great deal of anger towards her it brought about the beginnings of a change in his behavior towards Meg.

Some might say that the dragon symbol for girls is a *wish* for safety, a fantasy of protection in a world that is so unsafe for females. This alone might make it an important symbol, one that has the power to keep the girl's sense of self intact despite her surroundings. But for both girls and boys it is much more than a pretense (Figure 13.1).

*Figure 13.1 Dragon as guardian*

As the boy struggles with his dragon he learns self-control, self-respect and potentially respect for the forces of life around him and within him. As the girl brings forth her dragon and declares her ownership of and power over it, she, too, learns self-respect. She also discovers that she is powerful, regardless of how much the male-dominated world may limit this power.

The dragon may rise up out of the earth or the sea or descend on a gust of wind from the heavens. The dragon's arrival portends the opportunity for deep transformation in the child's psyche as it creates harmony or havoc in the sand scene or fantasy being described.

I used to find the image of Saint George slaying the dragon very upsetting. Why slay something that seemed to represent the very life force itself? But after many years of working with children and observing the use of this symbol I came to see that there are dragons and there are dragons. Some need to be slain. Some represent the life force turned on the self, the wild forces of nature run amok in the child's psyche. This is especially true of children such as Jacob whose parents have been battling for years. The radiant energy of the slain dragon is then available to the child. Like the giant bear in Chapter 1, the child can use the slain dragon as nourishment, and in so doing become the dragon. Much of life seems to require the acceptance of paradoxes such as this.

One very young boy's parents had been fighting so much that it had impacted his body, making it very hard for him to defecate. His bowels had become impacted and surgery seemed imminent. In his first session he made a scene in which a number dragons were eating babies. Some were being roasted first and others eaten alive. A group of soldiers stood by watching. It was a gruesome scene. In his next visit the same scene was repeated but then a wolf came and attacked the dragons and ate them. The fury of the wolf as he tossed the dragons into the air was very cathartic. The child was releasing all the pent-up anger and fear that he had been forced to eat during his parents' battles. His stomach rumbled as he played this scene out. His bowels were waking up. Later on the dragons came back to life as a force of nature aligned with the child, but he needed to slay them first, just as Jacob has done.

In Ursula LeGuin's *The Earthsea Trilogy*, the hero of the books, Ged, must harness the power of the dragon by learning its true name. In the process Ged must slay a few dragons or else perish. But he ultimately becomes aligned with them and they help each other as a result of this alignment. The book also tells us that dragons speak a language that we humans once knew long ago. It was our first language and children have some memory of it still. This sense of dragons as "the ancient ones" fits with how children use them, speak of them and benefit from them (LeGuin 1984).

On many trips to Greece I noticed that the dragon symbol was often a central figure in the Greek Orthodox churches I visited. These dragons were not being slain, as in the famous icon of Saint George and the Dragon, but were often covering the iconostasis, the elaborate wooden screen that separates the church from the altar in these churches, and behind which the mysteries of communion take place. Other dragons were depicted holding up icons or in other obviously central positions. I often inquired why the dragon was there and was often told that it represented sin, or the Pagan gods that Christianity had replaced, but this was clearly not the case. These dragons were alive and vital to whatever was to take place within those churches. The dragon ruled. Years later when I was studying the Greek language with a monk at a Greek Orthodox monastery near my home, I asked again about these dragons and was told unequivocally that they represented "the risen Christ." This made sense – again, the spirit of revolution, the life force.

With adults the provocation for change usually comes from outside of us – a crisis in a marriage or one's physical health or a confrontation or interpretation from one's therapist. Children, however, usually create their own provocation. The child intuitively senses "something is wrong with this picture" and goes about changing it or introducing an element which fosters change. The dragon does just this.

In this capacity the dragon is like a spark or glowing ember that illuminates or ignites the psyche. Here the element of fire enters in, the one we most often associate with dragons. Yet the dragon embodies all four elements, all four directions. Its role may be diverse but ultimately it serves the same purpose – that of empowerment and health. The following story was told spontaneously to me by a seven-year-old girl at the onset of her therapy with me:

> Once upon a time there lived a big, big dragon and that dragon was very nice because it never blew fire at people that he knew. But when he did blow fire that spot would turn to gold. So every day the dragon blew some fire and they all got some gold.
>
> But one day the dragon ran out of fire. And everybody went hungry. Everyone had to lose his or her houses and move to a different land. But the big dragon went back to the fire-breathing place and tried to get some more fire. And he could not get any.
>
> So another dragon that was very young took his place. Because this dragon had way more fire in him than none. So this baby dragon ran to the place where the people were going and stood right in their way.
>
> And everyone moved back because they thought this was an evil one. Then everyone watched him blow fire and saw that it turned into gold. And this young dragon was very special. This dragon could stay the way it was forever and never run out of fire, unless it had to be dead.

Dragons swoop down into children's play configurations on a very regular basis, or else they emerge from under the sand, their primal energy demanding recognition and often action of some sort. This may differ from child to child, and certainly from boys to girls, but its power is always pivotal.

The dragon is again a symbol of necessary revolution and the birth of a new order. It is also a vibrant symbol of wholeness. To me it symbolizes the entire process of working therapeutically with children. It arises when the child begins to reconnect with his or her deeper self. The child uses it to infuse the self with aliveness and to proclaim this life force. Children stand in awe of the symbol even though they themselves have created it. The dragon is fantastic and terrifying, wonderful and hideous, familiar and mysterious, very much like life itself.

## Acknowledgment

This chapter is based in part on an article by Dennis McCarthy (1997), "Awakening the dragon in children," *Psychological Perspectives 35*, 102–109.

# Chapter 14

# Mothers and Fathers

Holistic medicine, with its focus on health as opposed to illness, and its sometime creative use of symptoms, has many implications in the field of psychology as well. As we strengthen the physical immune system so that it can better stave off and process through illness, we may also consider how we might strengthen the psychic immune system, which parallels the physiological one and encompasses it.

Psychology is still too quick to diagnose, label and pathologize. In doing so we miss the person. The person is not the label or the diagnosis. In many ways the diagnosis is not real. It is a candle in the dark at best – an attempt to shed light on the mystery of human existence. The small amount that becomes visible via the lamp of psychological inquiry may enable us to help the person, but only if we remember that it is a small part that we are seeing. Otherwise it simply blinds us further.

Psyche means "soul" and psychology thus means the study of the soul. Keeping in mind that soul means the animating and vital principle in man credited with the faculties of thought, action and emotion we can view psychology as a potential doorway into a very different world than that of the narrow-minded clinician or therapist. The word *soul* is truly beautiful. It prescribes as well as describes what a life must entail or attempt to entail if it is worth living.

I offer these thoughts as a prelude to talking about mothers and fathers, who have been conspicuously absent from these pages. I have wanted to illuminate the experience of children on a psychic and energetic level, as well as the transformative process of play therapy, without focusing on the families these children are a part of. Too little is known and understood about what a child is, separate from their family system. Too often the implication is that our parents are responsible for all of our struggles, as we are nothing more than their mistakes or successes. But the child is born a separate although dependent being. An overemphasis on the power of the parent renders the child less powerful. Most of the children I work with have made huge changes often with their parents making very few. That said, I do want to stress the obvious significance our parents have on us, on both a personal and archetypal level (Figure 14.1).

*Figure 14.1 "Harry the broken-hearted monster": an eight-year-old boy in the midst of his parents' divorce*

When I first began to have children draw themselves as monsters many, many years ago, I assumed they were depicting an experience of or a response to their parents, an image of the huge form and force that parents seem to small children. I was made aware early on in my practice how large we are to the very young child. We are giants at a time when our children are most vulnerable, most impressionable. We rarely appreciate this fact and often feel a need to exaggerate our stature, especially if we are insecure in our role as parents. We have monsters lurking in our depths, usually ones we are unacquainted with, and thus our children become acquainted with them via our fear and anger.

I am amazed at how common it is for children to fear infanticide on the part of one or both of their parents. Many years ago, while I was reading Dorothy Bloch's (1994) book *So the Witch Won't Eat Me: The Child's Fear of Infanticide*, as it lay on the desk in my office every child that came for those few weeks asked me the name of the book, then asked me what infanticide meant. Usually children never noticed what books I read, as there are too many other more interesting objects in the room. After I rather tenuously told them what infanticide meant they all said that they had felt this fear with their own parents. It amazed me as the parents whose children I was working with at that time were for the most part loving and attentive. Yet each child shared this seemingly primal fear.

Bloch's premise is based on the myth of Oedipus just as Freud's central tenet of the Oedipal complex was. But Bloch looks at the first part of the myth that Freud seemed to overlook. When Oedipus is born his parents leave him on a hillside to die, abandoning him in the hopes of escaping their fates. By believing he is dead they actually seal their fate, and unconsciously bring about their own demise. Bloch felt, based on her work with children, that most children with serious emotional problems experience this abandonment and threat of death (Bloch 1994).

I believe this is true, that our attempts at avoiding ourselves may force our children to pay the price. This said, I still find that the monsters children imagine from early on are their own, not simply a response to their parents and their parents' monsters. Their monsters may come to be influenced by this imagined child-killing trait in their parents, a reaction in part to these giants who do have the power of life and death over us when we are small. But the monster, in its earliest forms especially, belongs to the child.

Too many theorists and therapists have gleaned their information on childhood only from adults remembering their childhoods or the detached observation of children by individuals who look with preconceived notions and who often seem to not even like children. In letting children begin to teach us about childhood we can then begin to consider how to better parent and teach the child. Margaret Lowenfeld, who created sandplay therapy in the early 1920s, was inspired to do so after reading a book by H.G. Wells called *Floor Games* (2004). In it he described a game he and his sons played on the floor in which they defined a specific area usually using blocks, and within this area they would create worlds, either everyday or fantastic. He observed that these experiences left him and his sons feeling very enlivened. Lowenfeld, perhaps in part because she grew up without a father, was deeply moved by this notion. The book was very controversial, as it was seen in Victorian England as an abomination that a father should play with his sons. The book was quickly pulled from circulation, but the seed had been planted in Lowenfeld's fertile and child-friendly mind, and she developed a method using a sandbox and what she called her "wonder box" which was filled with small objects for assembling in the sand into what she called "worlds." She also assumed that a child's associations with the various images they chose were central to the scenes meaning to them (Lowenfeld 1993). She was strongly criticized at the time for assuming the child could know about what had meaning to them, but her technique lasted and evolved and is ever increasing in use today. I love the fact that this very important method of helping children, and the centerpiece of my work, originated from a man playing on the floor with his two sons, a sign of the importance of play within the context of family if there ever was one.

I have also wanted to stress the importance of play, not just for the growing and the troubled child, but their parents as well. Joseph Chilton Pearce in *Evolution's End* speaks of play as:

> the foundation of creative intelligence, but like any intelligence, it must be developed; in keeping with nature's model-imperative, the child who is played with will learn to play. The child who is not played with will be unable to play and will be at risk on every level. (Pearce 1992, p.154)

By playing with the child and believing in its importance, we are sending a very powerful message to the parents of this child. I involve parents in the therapeutic process in a variety of ways but the most important function of parents' play is to allow for and anticipate change in the child and in them as a result. It is not only the child who emerges from this therapeutic process looking more alive and empowered. For a variety of reasons parents change alongside their children, not the least of which is that they feel relieved and more positive about their role as parents.

I find that very few parents value their role as mothers and fathers enough if at all. Psychoanalytic literature in many ways did a disservice to parents. First it focused almost exclusively on the role of the mother, laying the onus of responsibility for emotional disturbances on women. The reaction to this burden was initially guilt and fear but has ultimately been replaced by the outright rejection of the value, primariness and beauty of motherhood.

Fathers, on the other hand, in not being given enough responsibility by therapists, have been disempowered and left feeling insignificant. Most fathers I meet in my practice have no real appreciation of the potential positive (and negative) power they have over their children's lives. Most received inadequate fathering themselves and had fathers who did not realize how important they were to their children.

There is a thrust today not to say anything that might make parents feel guilty. Yet guilt and the remorse that it allows us to feel is a function of having a conscience, a reflection of our humanity. There is no way of avoiding this if we are to truly help our children. Being a parent brings with it the likelihood of making enormous mistakes. Yet it also contains the power to guard, guide and nurture. If we cannot or will not feel remorse, our capacity to love the child (or anyone) is diminished.

With the positive power of motherhood and fatherhood so devalued, it is no wonder that so many parents neglect their children's needs, allowing them to be raised by disinterested caretakers or television sets or video games, with which there can be no healthy bond.

I encourage parents when I first meet them to begin to open the doors to their own monsters. Some have already done so, but many have no awareness of their own interiors. As a result the basic premise of children's emotional needs and the causes of childhood problems are a total mystery to them. I begin working with a child by meeting with their parents or parent alone. At this first meeting I ask each parent what it would be like if they were a child and had themselves as a parent. For many parents this allows them to consider what they look like and how they feel to the child. The obstacles we create for our children out of our own fears become readily apparent when we reverse places.

Parents who are very narcissistic will be unable to answer this question as it is not in keeping with the image of themselves they have. It is after all very difficult for most of us to admit that we have failed with our children. Yet if we can be honest with ourselves the possibility for change arises. More than anything I attempt in my first meeting with parents to provoke in them the desire to deepen their understanding of themselves, of their psyches and psychic processes. Sometimes I share the following experience with them.

Many years ago I was referred a family whose six-year-old daughter had been waking up with night terrors for many years. The parents had tried everything, from having her sleep in their bed with them, to tranquilizers, but to no avail. They came alone to see me, without their daughter. I asked each of them if anything terrifying had ever happened to them, if their own childhoods in particular had contained much or anything that evoked terror. The mother began to weep and spoke of her early years, which were fraught with great deprivation and loneliness. I mentioned that it would be fruitful for her and her daughter if she pursued a course of therapy to sort out all this buried pain she was referring to.

She waited a year before taking my advice, but from the day of our initial meeting, in which she acknowledged her own terror, her daughter never woke up again at night. I never actually saw the child. The symptoms stopped, and as in the rest of her life she seemed well adjusted she never came for a session. The child had been expressing her mother's unconscious terror. Although this was my first experience of a child expressing a parent's emotions for them, it was not the last. In this case, by simply peeking into the previously unopened door, the child was freed from the grip of the mother's pain.

In the *Inner World of Childhood*, Francis Wickes (1978) elaborates on this psychic bond between parent and child. At first the child has an infinitesimal conscious. The states of consciousness are fleeting impressions attached to no central or ego sense. There is no continuity of memory. Slowly these fragments begin to integrate and a sense of self develops. The child begins to think of himself as something separate from his surroundings. The "I" emerges; a personal life slowly takes form. At first the child is in a condition of identity with the psyche of the parent. Even as the "I" emerges, the unconscious is still held in that close identification.

We recognize the physical and economic dependence of the child upon the father and mother. We do not attach sufficient importance to the psychic bond that in early childhood often amounts to a condition of identity of the unconscious of the child with the unconscious of the parent (Wickes 1978).

Wickes is not proposing a tabula rasa or "blank slate" theory, but simply saying that when the umbilical cord is cut the psychic cord is not. The more we know ourselves, examining our own *inner* selves especially, the less negative influences this material will have on our children.

Eight-year-old Lisa was extremely bright and verbal. She came for therapy in the midst of her parents' separation, with numerous physical complaints. Her parents suspected those symptoms were related to how Lisa felt about the separation, which she was not expressing to them. This was only partly true.

In meeting with Lisa she presented a dichotomy. She was extremely clear about her negative feelings and quite an aggressive, extroverted child inside. But her external countenance and behavior belied this. She acted very "proper," like a little adult. Her parents were very proud of these qualities in Lisa. Little did they suspect the pain and conflict they were causing her. What became clear was that Lisa felt imprisoned by the false manner in which she related to the world. She was convinced she had to do so to spare her parents. To spare her parents *what* you might ask? Her sessions were energetic and a great deal of anger and creativity came out, which did alleviate her symptoms. But in school and at home she still *acted* and this bothered her immensely.

Lisa shared a recurrent dream with me at the onset of her therapy. "I am lying down and someone is smothering me by forcing something sickeningly sweet down my throat. I hate it and try to scream but I can't." In Lisa's dream she is describing the act of introjecting or absorbing her parents' repression. Both parents were ministers and admittedly felt a need to act "sickeningly sweet" to their congregations. They felt that they had to be paragons of perfection, and their daughter felt this unspoken requirement as well. There was enormous pressure on them from within and without. They in turn fed this to Lisa in all of their interactions. She acquiesced to spare them their own fury. Often a repressive atmosphere in the home does more damage to the child than the specific mistakes that parents make. Fortunately Lisa at eight recognized that this was not her. She used the image from her recurrent dream in creative, cathartic play to alter her inner state. This resulted in her feeling much better and her parents feeling worse. They had been denying how miserable they were. Lisa, by refusing to carry this misery for them, forced them to deal with it. This in turn resulted in them changing their own life situations for the better. Lisa dreamt for her parents as well as herself.

I urge parents to consider if any experiences from their own past parallel or in any way correlate to the child's problems or emotional state. One mother took this question home with her and it sat in the back of her mind for many weeks while I began a fairly successful treatment of her son. One night in a dream she began to remember a long period of sexual abuse she had experienced as a child and which she had willfully and successfully forgotten at age 12. She was able to see the many physical and psychological effects these repressed memories had had on her life, as well as on her son's life. He was the only male she had ever trusted and loved since her childhood and as a result his own psyche absorbed the material repressed within hers. This was certainly true of the other mother mentioned earlier.

Often if our hearts are broken or closed when we are little, it is our children who become the recipients of the feelings surrounding these wounds, either in the manner described above or by their provocation of anger in us that is much more intense than the situation merits. In these cases just the acknowledgment alone of the projected part of us frees the child from it. Of course, seeking help to deal with and resolve it makes sense and would further assure that our child remains unburdened of it.

In David Sobel's wonderful book *Children's Special Places* (1993) he explores the cross-cultural tendency of children, especially during latency, to create special places for themselves, such as forts, dens, and bush houses. He emphasizes the important developmental function of these special places.

He bases his ideas in part on the work of Joseph Chilton Pearce. In Pearce's schema the child progresses through a series of matrixes (Latin for womb) during pre-adolescent development. The first matrix is the actual womb, the second is mother and the third is earth. Each matrix is a sphere with the earlier matrixes contained within each subsequent one. Each matrix is the significant world or safe place in which the individual resides, a source of energy and a place from which to explore out into the world, most specifically the subsequent matrix (Sobel 1993).

If we keep in mind the child's need to separate themselves from their parents, both physically and psychically, these special places are then an attempt to do so, created and inhabited in the spirit of play. It is this spirit in which all growth and learning happen for the child.

The child is literally grounded through and by their mother initially. Through playful explorations and forays out into the world of earth, the child begins to ground themselves in themselves, thus becoming able to meet many of their own needs. Each phase of growth is like a womb from which the next phase is born. The self, too, once the child possesses it and embodies it, is womb-like, giving rise to all of our creative thoughts and actions. Through play we see children learning this self-regulation. The need for play is an essential component of childhood.

Sandplay offers a miniature version of these forts or special spaces, as it is a chance for children to create a world that they are in charge of. It isn't as satisfying as climbing into that world in the way children can do with a small fort made of blankets and pillows or a hut in the woods made of simple leaning sticks, but because of the bodily way that children experience sandplay it does have a similar effect. The four walls of the sandbox and the playroom's defined boundaries give the entire experience that of a "special place."

Several times when I have encountered children I work with while walking in a nearby street, they acted shocked at my being there. "What are you doing out here?" several of them said. "Get back inside quick!" One six-year-old simply put his head against my belly and began to push me backwards towards my office. I got the point. I was the guardian of the space and the special world they had created in it. I was associated with this world and it alone, and I must have seemed almost like a recurrent dream figure, suddenly come to life to them in another place. It reminded me of the powerful otherworldliness of the play experience.

With all the body consciousness that we as adults and parents in recent years profess to have acquired, we seem to still mainly see the outside, that is, how we look rather than how we feel. And if we are aware of our children on a body level it is in this same shallow way. We worry about things such as "Are they obese?" "Do they fit in?" "Are they dressed trendy enough?" How often do we ask "What did you dream about last night?" or "How do you feel?" or "What frightens you most about life?"

Parents take yoga classes and work out in gyms, but at the same time (sometimes literally at the same time) they plop their children in front of computers to play ultra-violent video games for ever-increasing amounts of their lives. In both the adult and the child, the need for creativity is undervalued. There is no time for the hurried adult to engage in truly creative acts. When their children are not in front of a video screen they are being rushed to numerous activities that are more about the external form, looking good in the eyes of others, and not for the child. Or they are left to their own devices, ignored unless the child gets in trouble and then the child is held responsible, or the violent culture we live in, not our own blind, self-centeredness. Our children are left alone with their wildness, with their monsters. So much in children's lives encourages the suppression of both wildness and monster. Through our silence we encourage them to ignore their rich interiors. Meanwhile the wild beast within is rip-snorting mad at being neglected. Again, this beast appears to us as symptoms: phobias, depressions, attention difficulties, addictions, eating disorders, rages and myriad other disturbing forms.

All the adults in a child's life, parents, teachers, lawyers, judges, pediatricians, etc., and all of a child's peers to some extent, have monsters within in the form of big feelings that are unexpressed, unresolved and unconscious. Most run from this bigness rather than seeing it as the beacon it should be. The greatest gift we can give our children is to make every effort to encounter the monstrous feelings within ourselves, and the bigness of life they arise from and attempt to describe. Just the effort to do so brings about a change.

Second, we should encourage our children, students, friends, clients, etc. to be honest and real. How many teachers tolerate let alone encourage honesty and realness? Most teachers are psychologically unaware. Keeping in mind that knowledge is an extension of a person's ability to differentiate, to say no, honesty does indeed have a central place in the classroom, as well as the home.

Refusal to admit the truth about our lives, our experiences, keeps us imprisoned despite efforts to free ourselves through material possessions, drugs, overwork, or the myriad means by which people run away from or attempt to rise above their deeper feelings. Although it is too late for us as adults to have "a happy childhood," it is never too late to grieve what we have lost, and in so doing breathe life into our spirits – dragon breath.

A man I recently worked with had been terribly abused by his father as a boy and suffered without knowing why as an adult from this. Slowly via therapy he began to remember what had happened to him. In one session he suddenly said in a loud voice, "He killed me! He killed the little boy that I was!" It surprised him because it was a different voice he was using, a different part of himself he was speaking from. Then he said it again and again, many times, and began weeping deeply as he did so.

When he finally stood up after the storm of his sorrow had subsided, he looked incredible, upset but renewed. His eyes were soft and open – *seeing* for the first time in years. His face was flushed. His whole demeanor was infused with life. In speaking the truth he began to resurrect the slain child within, which allowed him to truly come back to life. That night he dreamt that he was dancing in an underground chamber, feeling more alive and happy than he had ever remembered feeling. It was a long and ecstatic dance, and when he awoke he felt like a new man. He went on to quit his job as a high-powered trial lawyer, which he had taken to make his father happy, and found a direction that was his own heart's choice.

If a man in his forties benefited so much from truth, how much more will our children benefit from our honesty. One other story comes to mind, which I sometimes share with parents and often tell myself. It is very old and I believe it is attributed to the Taoist master Chuang Tzu:

> A sea bird was spotted in a certain inland province of China. This bird, rare and exotic in these parts, was brought to the attention of the ruler of the province. Delighted and honored by the bird's presence, he ordered great delicacies to be fed to it, musicians to play for it; that is, it was treated in a way that a human would appreciate, not a sea bird. And the bird wasted away and died as a result.

To see who our children are and nurture them according to their own needs, not ours, is certainly the only way to raise them. Yet how to do this, and not assume we know them as extensions of us? The symbolic-energetic therapy process elaborated on in these pages has as its main goal the reinstatement of the child's ability to say what they want and need, hopefully facilitating their parents' ability concomitantly to accommodate and make room for this.

When the dreamer alluded to in this book's beginning who envisioned a huge monster in his childhood house or when anyone longing for wholeness is finally able to open the door and resolve and/or embody the feelings therein, then the whole house will be his to walk through, in freedom and peace.

# Epilogue
## In the Footsteps of Pan

For many years I have been trying to understand what is happening in the play therapy process that facilitates transformation, in the hopes of better understanding the child and life itself as a result. I am still always surprised by play's efficacy, always startled by the ways in which it helps children to change. As part of this inquiry, I have explored play as a form-altering process that allows for the disorganization and reorganization that is needed for deep change to occur. I have examined the effects play has on the body and the energetic experience of the child engaged in it. In regards to sandplay, I have explored the use of the sand's depth and its physical qualities, looking at the use of the material itself, minus all the pictorial possibilities that figures offer. I have been continually interested in fostering ways of accessing instinctual energy and experiencing the body and the psyche in all its fullness.

I have also explored several images that arise in the sandplay process with great frequency and relevance. This has led me to the realms of the dragon and then the serpent, all images of life at its deepest. The children and adults I work with responded by using these images with increasing frequency and poignancy as I examined their meanings. I have always been clear about the personal interest I have in these aspects of play and the unconscious, knowing that if it has meaning for me personally and I explore this and utilize this aspect I will be better able to understand its meaning to the child. In this manner it becomes a collaborative effort, inspiring my self-exploration and theirs in rich and creative ways.

Right now the god Pan is calling me with his panic-inducing flute music and once again the response has been interesting in my sessions and in my own dreams, as well as those of people I treat. Pan is the most elusive of the gods. Very little is known about him and very few stories are associated with him in Greek myth, and yet he has inspired more stories, appeared in more literature, than any other god. His name is the root of more words in our language than any other deity. He is ever present and influential and yet mysterious and unknown.

His lineage is confusing, with numerous males claiming to be his father. His mother was probably a nymph, but here too mythic history is vague. He was presented as an orphan to the gods on Mount Olympus, wrapped in the skin of a rabbit, and from the start he made the gods laugh and they loved him for this. It is interesting that he who made the gods laugh makes us panic.

The pre-classical roots of Pan are very ancient. As he is part animal and the god of all nature, he must have arisen from a time when people lived as one with the world of nature. The god of the flocks, of springs and grottos as well as mountaintops, he is associated with unfettered sexuality and with creativity, two aspects of the same energy. He became the prototype of the devil with the advent of Christianity and the early Christian fathers sent him underground, leaving him for dead, while they were busy lopping off the genitals of male statues or covering them with fig leaves. They could not tolerate sexuality, unable to see its godliness.

Yet Pan remained alive. The image of "the green man" appeared in architecture at about that time, embedded in numerous Christian churches throughout Europe. These images of the green man, often horned and sprouting leaves and tendrils from his mouth, grew in numbers through the Romanesque period and especially in the Gothic period: "The green man signifies irrepressible life. He appears and seems to die and then comes again after long forgettings. In all of his appearances he is an image of renewal and rebirth" (Anderson 1990, p.14). Regarding the supposed death of Pan, a cry went through late antiquity – "The Great God Pan is dead!"

> Nature had become deprived of its creative voice. It was no longer an independent living force of generativity. What had had soul, lost it: or lost was the psychic connection to nature... Nature no longer spoke to us – or we could no longer hear. The person of Pan the mediator, like an aether who invisibly enveloped all natural things with personal meaning, with brightness, had vanished. Stones became stones – trees, trees; things, places and animals no longer were this god or that... When Pan is alive then nature is too, and it is filled with gods, so that the owl's hoot is Athena and the mollusk on the shore is Aphrodite. These bits of nature are not merely attributes or belongings. They are the gods in their biological forms. (Hillman 1979, p.xxiii)

Most children are innately polytheistic, or really pantheistic, seeing not just many gods, but god in everything. One of the great powers of the sandplay process is that through it we offer many figures that may hold this deified energy as we also offer the earth itself in the form of sand. During early childhood, through latency and even into adolescence this pantheistic tendency continues. As the child sits by the sandbox or sandtray, they are open to the endless possibilities that the imagination offers. They are sitting to some degree before all of nature. They are in the realm of Pan. They may plant new ways of being in this fertile imaginal soil. They may create typhoons and volcanic eruptions that change the form of everything, both inside and out. They create, destroy and recreate and believe in it all (Figure E.1).

*Figure E.1 An eight-year-old girl depicts herself safe in the arms of a tree monster near the end of her therapy*

Pan appears in *The Wind in the Willows* as a protector of small creatures. The central characters follow his song and enter into his presence much as children follow the lead of their own deeper instincts in therapeutic play:

> A great Awe fell upon him, an awe that turned his muscles to water, bowed his head and rooted his feet to the ground. It was no panic terror – indeed he felt wonderfully at peace and happy – but it was an awe that smote and held him and, without seeing he knew it could only mean that some august Presence was very, very near. (Grahame 1983, p.126)

Pan enters the therapy space, the sandbox, and the child's imaginative play as the great initiator of change. That is his function. He forces change by moving us from where we stand rooted so that we unsettle until we are in a new and hopefully better place. In *The Crock of Gold* by James Stephens, Pan appears at the story's beginning and instigates change. Once he has upset the equilibrium of everyone's lives, he leaves. His job is done. The book's main character, Caitlin, is lured from the stifling safety of her father's house by the sound and energy of Pan's flute. She follows Pan up into the hills "because he was naked and unashamed" (Stephens 1969, p.46). Once she has begun her journey and been initiated by Pan, he moves on, replaced by new energy, new challenges. Once we have fled in terror or leapt into the air with delight, the god moves on. I look for Pan to show up where stasis rules. He may take many forms but he always brings new and needed creative energy that actually originates from within the individual. His music elicits it, lures it to the surface, but it is the energy of the listener, the seeker, the panicked one.

Jung, in his book *The Archetypes and the Collective Unconscious*, speaks of the transformative power of "immediate experience" (Jung 1959). By this he is talking about an experience that is not brought on by ritual or intention but simply a spontaneous, ecstatic or visionary experience. Sandplay offers a perfect setting for this, as does the child's natural predilection towards this immediacy. I have witnessed and helped foster many sessions in which this spontaneous, transformative moment occurred. With a palpable rush of energy that makes one's hair stand on end if we are really present to it, Pan enters the room. As I write these lines, a child came to see me and made the following scene:

> A wall separates the land of men and the land of Wildness. But the land of Wildness contains a great treasure, a gem that has "all knowledge within it." It sits at the bottom of a deep watering hole, guarded by a five-headed serpent. Many wild animals, such as elephants and wolves and lions, approach the watering hole to drink from it, and as they near it they go into a trance that makes them ferocious, wanting to protect the treasure. The encampment of soldiers seeking the treasure is very close to the watering hole also. It is as if two parallel universes or realities have suddenly come close to each other. The animals began to leap over the dividing wall to attack the men. Meanwhile, a shepherd lives in a small house in the midst of the Wildness. He has been living there for so very long that he has become one with the animals. He is hiding to protect himself from the battle.

The over-intellectualized boy who made the above scene was struggling successfully, with my help and his parents' permission, to explore and integrate
the repressed parts of himself that had manifested instead in chronic anxiety
and periodic explosions. He made the above scene after talking about the
enormous pressure he put on himself to be the best at everything and "to not
rock the boat." He wept freely as he spoke and then after blowing his nose
made this scene. He was thrilled with it. He emphasized the depth of the
watering hole and the fierce guardianship of the five-headed beast, lest I not
appreciate these points. He left the session a greatly relieved, more self-
possessed child.

I thought about his watering hole after he left. The watering hole is a
rich image, a place of sustenance and also of intense animal energy. It is really
a great image for the entire dynamic play therapy process, in which the
sandbox and all the many play materials, combined with the child's
body-based imagination, render the space a watering hole. I worked with a
child who spent part of each year in South Africa with her father and who
described the watering holes she had seen on safari. She often made scenes
of these watering holes and came to use the image in her therapy to
overcome some deep fear that was manifesting in recurring nightmares and
as frequent illnesses. For her the watering hole was seen as a place of safety
and healing. When she imagined herself near them with all the wild animals
she felt whole. The watering hole is a form of "the deep well" that Jung spoke
of.

I have read that at the premier showing of Jean Cocteau's movie version
of the classic French tale *Beauty and the Beast*, the actress Marlene Dietrich was
in the audience. At the end, when the Beast turns into the Prince, she is said
to have stood up and shouted out, "My Beast, give me back my Beast!" I
don't know if this is a true story but it is a wonderful one. By the movie's end,
the Beast is somehow closer to our hearts than the Prince. Perhaps Beauty
can't really wed the Beast as the Beast, cannot live with him as such, but we
miss his wildness, his earthiness. We recognize it as a great loss. If this
wildness is too buried it will emerge as shadow, as negative or even abusive
behavior. How to keep this wild self closer to the surface where we can use
it? How to let it live in us, and become the source of creativity that it can be?
The Beast has been Beauty's salvation. He would be ours perhaps if we could
only find him again.

Pan is the most bestial of the Greek gods. Half man and half goat, in
statues he seems to be embedded in the animal world, beckoning us to him
and repelling us at the same time. Pan seems like this missing piece of our

consciousness. He has been missing for a long, long time but the need to find him, to listen to his flute playing, is more imperative than ever. The children we see in therapy and all children live in a world that is at risk on many levels. Many therapists and educators make the mistake of not seeing the children they work with in the context of this world, limiting their concerns with family systems and diagnosis. But children are very influenced by the world around them, as well as the ever-present ancient history of humanity. The same mind set that plops children down in front of a computer for most of each day and especially during weekends and vacations is the mind set that allows for global warming, disregarding the ways in which we must change to keep the earth alive. It is the same mind set that concerns itself with how our children look on the outside but totally disregards their insides.

Pan is old, very old, not simply antediluvian but much older still. He is an archetype of our first human form, an image of us as we evolved from the animal world. He has the power and mystery of something deeper than is fathomable. We can hardly take him in, as our consciousness rebels against the very ancientness of him. We can't encounter him directly. We can only look around for evidence of his footprints.

Many years ago I was hiking with a friend on a remote mountain in Italy. It was midday, the time of Pan, and we sat by a spring and listened to the hum of the cicadas. We both fell into a daze. Time stood still. At some point one of us noticed hundreds of hoofprints in the mud around the edge of the spring. It was wild boar! Remembering the last time I had seen one of those huge, tusked beasts, we quietly but swiftly roused ourselves and made our way down the mountain. I still savor not only those moments of sun-dazed idleness but especially the panic I felt on seeing the prints of the beasts. I felt that I'd had a glimpse of eternity.

Jung spoke of the two-million-year-old man that lives deep in all of us as the seat and source of wisdom. He saw therapy and life as an effort to connect or reconnect with this wisdom. This can only happen if we push beyond the known into the natural world of the instincts and the realm of the imagined. The power of play is its replication of the natural world, its use of the imagination to envision it and the possibility it offers of "immediacy." If we are lucky, Pan surprises us with his presence, his footsteps leading us closer to the bigness of life.

# References

Anderson, W. (1990) *Green Man: Archetype of Oneness with the Earth*. London: HarperCollins.

Baker, E.F. (1967) *Man in the Trap*. New York: Collier.

Bloch, D. (1994) *So the Witch Won't Eat Me: The Child's Fear of Infanticide*. Lanham, MD: Jason Aaronson.

Erikson, E. (1950) *Childhood and Society*. New York: Norton.

Erikson, E. (1977) *Toys and Reason*. New York: Norton.

Grahame, K. (1983) *The Wind in the Willows*. New York: Simon & Schuster.

Graves, R. (1983) *The Myths of the Greeks*. New York: Penguin.

Hillman, J. (1979) *Pan and the Nightmare*. New York: Spring Publications.

Johnson, R.A. (1991) *Owning Your Own Shadow*. San Francisco: Harper.

Joyce, J. (1986) *Ulysses (The Gabler Edition)*. New York: Vintage.

Jung, C.G. (1959) *The Archetypes and the Collective Unconscious*. New York: Bollingen Foundation.

Jung, C.G. (1961) *The Collected Works of C.G. Jung*. New York: Bollingen Foundation.

Kalff, D.M. (1980) *Sand Play*. Boston: Sigo Press.

LeGuin, U. (1984) *The EarthSea Trilogy*. Toronto: Bantam.

Lewis, C.S. (1988) *Voyage of the Dawn Treader*. New York: Macmillan.

Lowen, A. (1970) *Pleasure: A Creative Approach to Life*. Harmondsworth: Penguin.

Lowen, A. (1972) "Horror: The Face of Unreality" *Lecture 1*. Urdorf-Zürich: Institute for Bioenergetic Analysis.

Lowen, A. (1990) *The Spirituality of the Body*. Basingstoke: Macmillan.

Lowenfeld, M. (1993) *Understanding Children's Sandplay*. Worksop: Lowenfeld Trust.

Pearce, J.C. (1992) *Evolution's End*. London: HarperCollins.

Perrault, C. (1961) *Perrault's Fairy Tales*. New York: Dodd, Mead.

Reich, W. (1945) *Character Analysis*. New York: Simon & Schuster.

Reich, W. (1973) *The Function of the Orgasm*. New York: Simon & Schuster.

Sendak, M. (1963) *Where the Wild Things Are*. New York: Harper & Row.

Singer, J. (1986) *The Unholy Bible*. Boston: Sigo Press.

Smith, C. (2007) *Ki, Chi, Blood, Lust and Warp Spasm*. Grandmaster magazine. Available at www.craigsmithcolumns.homesstead.com/warpspasm.html

Sobel, D. (1993) *Children's Special Places*. Chicago: Zephyr Press.

Stassinopoulos, A. (1983) *The Gods of Greece*. New York: Abrams.

Stephens, J. (1969) *The Crock of Gold*. London: Macmillan.

Stevens, A. (1983) *Archetypes*. New York: William Morrow.

*Webster's New World Dictionary*. (1970) New York: The World Publishing Co.

Wells, H.G. (2004) *Floor Games: A Father's Account of Play and Its Legacy of Healing*. Ed. B. Turner. Cloverdale, CA: Temenos Press.

Wickes, F. (1978) *The Inner World of Childhood*. Boston: Sigo Press.

Winnicott, D.W. (1971) *Playing and Reality*. London: Tavistock.

# Recommended Reading

*Tales from Moominvalley* and *Moominland in November* by Tove Jansson. Farrar, Straus and Giroux: New York, 1995 (and any other of the Moomintroll books).

*The Golden Key* and *The Light Princess* by George MacDonald. Farrar, Straus and Giroux: New York, 1967.

*The Golden Compass, The Subtle Knife* and *The Amber Spyglass* by Phillip Pullman. Knopf: New York, 1996, 1997, 2000.

*The EarthSea Trilogy* and *Teanu* by Ursula LeGuin. Houghton Miffin: New York, 2005.

*The Neverending Story* by Michael Ende. Doubleday Books: New York, 1983.

*The Crock of Gold* by James Stephens. Macmillan: London, 1969.

# Index